THEY CALLED US

DARKIES

Based on the true story of Betty Jackson

THEY CALLED US
DARKIES

Based on the true story of Betty Jackson

By

THOMAS A. BRISCOE

Briscoe Book Publishing
Houston, Texas

THEY CALLED US
DARKIES

Published by:
Briscoe Book Publishing
Houston, Texas
Briscoe@grm.net

Thomas A. Briscoe, Publisher
Stephanie Briscoe, Editorial Director
Yvonne Rose/Quality Press.info, Book Packager
Cover Illustration by Sheron Smith

Copyright © 2021 by Thomas A. Briscoe

Paperback ISBN #: 978-1-7371841-1-9

Hardcover ISBN #: 978-1-7371841-2-6

Ebook ISBN #: 978-1-7371841-0-2

Library of Congress Control Number: 2021908936

Acknowledgements

To my aunt Betty, thank you for the many phone conversations you had with me throughout our years together, and for the countless stories told to me over and over again. Since I was a little girl, I have always felt your love and kindness towards me. I love you, and I will never forget you.

Secondly, I would like to thank my mother, June, for the hard work and dedication she put forth in attempting to treat all people equally, despite the challenges of pain and sorrow she must have tolerated during this trying period in her life. Mom you are a tough soul to have endured so much. I hope one day you will receive back all the love and happiness you gave to others while on this earth.

Lastly, I would also like to thank my uncle Larry Jackson, who supported me from the very beginning. God bless you.

The story of this book was produced from several interviews before Aunt Betty ascended to be with God. It is also a compilation of various stories I heard from her throughout the years.

This is an inspirational story about courage, and one young woman's determination to live through the everyday challenges her family faced and the struggles they overcame.

I hope, as you read this book, it touches your heart. Please realize that the pages of this book are written about a time period when racism prevailed over the true love of God in this Universe. Many men became drunken with evil deeds that would lurk to steal one's soul. Because of this, many people suffered. Not only did they suffer, they also perished.

For we look to discern the Light, but nevertheless will it shine...?
For we discern to find the Light, but shall it bring forth glory...?

-   *Stephanie D. Briscoe*

Contents

They Called Us Darkies

Introduction

There was a certain rich man, who was clothed in royal blue and fine linen, and lived with good treatment by others so that he resided in a place of comfort every day. And there was a certain beggar named Eleazar. This man did not have the entitlements of the rich man, but he lay at the magnificently-designed gate of the rich man, daily. He desired that perhaps the rich man would be nice to him by treating him equally. Moreover, he desired to be fed by him because he was hungry. The people belonging to the kingdom treated the beggar differently, also. Because the cast of his appearance looked most different from others belonging to the same kingdom, no one would help him. Day after day, Eleazar lay, resting, waiting for the rich man to pass by him. He would ask the rich man, "Could I at least have the leftover crumbs from your dinner table?" But the rich man showed no mercy. Over time, Eleazar developed sores on his body as sickness fell upon him from experiencing a hard life. Even the dogs would approach him and display more compassion in his affliction than the people. The dogs licked the wounds that covered his body to ease the pain. The rich man ignored the beggar's plea day after day and demanded the guards to take him away.

It came to pass, years later, that the beggar died. He was carried into heaven's resting area by the angels and, afterwards, placed in Abram's bosom. Later, the rich man died also and was buried. But, when the rich man opened his eyes a short time after death, he found himself in the middle of Hades. He existed still, however he now lived in the torments of hell. When he looked upwards to heaven, he saw that Eleazar was there resting in the arms of Abram. Being in agony because of the heat, he sought for Eleazar to dip his finger in water to cool his tongue, if but only for a moment. But Abram reminded the rich man, "Do you remember in thy lifetime when you were on the earth? You received the good things, such as favor and wealth, while Eleazar received only evil. Now he is comforted, but you are in torment. And, besides this, I cannot help you, because there is a large abyss fixed between us and the place where you are. So the people that are here cannot cross over to help you, neither can they that are with you come over here." Then the rich man said, "Therefore, I pray to thee to allow Eleazar to go back to the earth and find my family. I have five brothers and other family members. He needs to tell them about this place. Maybe if he comes back from the dead they will believe his warning! I don't want them to make the same mistake I have, and, when they die, they come to this place." But Abram said to him, "God has sent prophets on the earth to alert people by telling them about this place. This place is the consequence for all those that choose to hate rather than to love while living on the earth. This is the result for all those that choose to oppress others solely because of who they are." Then the rich man replied, "But if you would send a person back to the earth who they knew had died, they would believe it." Abram ends his discussion with, "If they do not care to believe the prophets that are sent by God, they will neither be persuaded, even if a person comes back from the dead."

****

The stories in this book are not aimed directly to discredit any specific ethnic groups of people, cultures, or religions. They only seek to open eyes and change destinies.

Thank you, and I hope you enjoy!

1

"A Murdered People"

In the damp darkness of the local county jail cell, Joshua Jackson slept. He lay on his back, arms folded on his chest, exhaling deep, long breaths. Snoring softly, he could not fully open his mouth for fear of awaking the guards on duty. He was a hardworking, large black man in the early 1900's whose relatives called him Euell. Learning to sleep, well, let's say anywhere, he was resting peacefully that night. Only the wind blowing the autumn leaves outside the high, barred window, and a few distant horses, could be heard.

Just then, the silence was broken by the clanging of keys. Pushing against the cell door, it opened... Three white men crept in. One with a shotgun positioned himself in the corner of the small cell furthest from the bed. Lifting the long barrel in a ready position, by his posture, you could tell he was prepared to kill. Jimmy, the heavy-set officer in charge, whispered to his deputy, "Get in front of him, Billy!"

Billy entered and planted his feet firmly in the center of the room. Jimmy moved in slowly around Billy and toward Joshua's bed with a 4"-by-4" piece of lumber at his side. The three men didn't want to awaken any of the other inmates in the jailhouse. Though murdering a black man in jail would hardly conjure up any form of a thorough investigation, they didn't want any complications. Most of all, they didn't want to fully awaken a man whose shoulders were too wide to comfortably fit on the steel bed that had no mattress or bedding. After all, what was the choice now... Finish the mission or be caught committing murder.

The three men checked their positions one last time with a quick nod of affirmation.

"Hey, Nigga'..." Billy muttered. But there was no movement. "Nigga'!" he spoke more loudly as he kicked the dirt floor with the heel of his boot. Just then, Joshua Jackson sat up, disoriented, trying to make out who had entered his jail cell. But, before he could focus, a crushing blow penetrated the top of his skull. Blood splattered across the cell and onto the dirt floor. For a split second, everyone was frozen. Jimmy had always been one of the town's most notorious citizens for showing no sympathy toward blacks. But now, even he, hands shaking, was second-guessing their decision. He hesitated for just an instant, then... Pow!!! Another blow shattered the back of Joshua's skull, sending him into a sprawled position of unconsciousness. One last exhale was heard as a long, slow stream of blood formed across the room.

"Steady, boys," Billy whispered, as they carried Joshua out of the jail cell.

"One less darky in this town," Jimmy muttered.

Another one gone in a shade darker than the night...

Things were different back then... back in the dawn of the 1900's. Joshua Euell Jackson was my great uncle, the uncle of my daddy. When my ancestors went to claim the body, one would think that the police would conjure up a story of how he had died while incarcerated in their jailhouse. But that would have been a little too kind. Rather it was more common for a good dose of mocking targeted towards one's God-given intelligence. Accompanied by a hate-filled racial murder, many black people, and even whites, looked the other way in fear they might be next, given it was often told around town, "Now, if anyone of y'all wants to take up for one of these darkies, we'll be visiting your home next!"

So an additional document of death, complete with cruel gloating, was handed to my family. In the space for "Cause of Death" it read: "Accidental death, Timber fell on his head." Although this document was optional for black folks, the county sheriff on that day made special arrangements to deliver it himself. This one was given, not to explain the cause for taking a human life in the county's jurisdiction... And, of course, not for legal purposes... No, this document was given to further drain a race of people emotionally, mentally, and spiritually as well. It was not enough to murder our loved one in cold blood. They had to diminish a family of any sense of justice. Anyway... that's how I feel. The purpose that day was to dishearten a family, to annihilate any sense of possible value, to destroy their future. There were even drops of dry blood on the death certificate as a permanent reminder of the act.

Such were the lives of the people that I came from. These stories I heard from ma and pa revealed that Uncle Josh could be belligerent when he drank at times. And smarting off to the policemen in town always made things worse for us black citizens. His real crime, though, was that he had been born black. By my recollection, white men could drink, be belligerent, and live, probably by sleeping it off without even the smallest warrant or arrest.

The wretched world of American slavery was still fresh, at least in the minds of many.

Manipulated as frequently and conveniently as possible, it was within every citizen's man-made psyche. The Emancipation Proclamation was lawful on paper. Murder was unlawful but only on paper. The double and triple standards prevailed off paper, as distinguishable as peasantry versus royalty from the white nations of old. The psychological art of keeping a race of People down was

5

ongoing. In my mind, as a young girl, I was most times wondering why many white folks back then seemed so angry, simply because I was here! Here on this earth! Hmmmm... I wonder...

The gray mule pulled the rickety wagon up the dirt road with Joshua's body laying face-up. His huge arms rested on top of his chest. My daddy held the reigns with Euell's wife and mom sitting in the front.

No tears flowed.

My daddy looked straight ahead. Two young boys sat in the back of the wagon. Being careful not to kick the body, they huddled together to pray. Town folks came out to watch the procession. Some looked sad, some shook their head, some smiled and whispered. But no one, black or white, shed a tear. *'Why cry for them?'* the white folks thought. *'Why cry in front of them?'* the black folk inwardly responded. Such evil meshed with such pride now took center stage in this dark cavalcade. The only sounds were the wagon's wheels moving, along with click-clacking hooves and a few heavy snorts from the mule.

Inside the tavern, there was music and laughter. Billy teased Jimmy while pouring him a drink. "I thought you said you was gonna' knock him dead with one hit..."

Another officer on duty leaned backward whispering to the bar clerk with a big grin on his face. "Hell, when ya' kill a wild boar, you get that last lick in just to make sure he's dead."

Sounds of laughter came from Billy, as Jimmy downed a shot of whisky from a slumped position in his chair. With a cowboy hat lowered beneath his eyes, Jimmy slowly lifted the brim and gazed around the room. He had no smile, just a wry, irritated smirk. "I don't know nothin' about hittin' no wild boars, but I do know how good it feels to kill me another nigger."

'*I am a damned good cop*,' Jimmy thought, as he poured Billy another beer.

I'm always sad in the back of my mind, and I try not to think about it. But inequality in America has always been an enemy to us. A hatred that stemmed from something as trivial as a man's skin color? Well, that topped the ridiculousness of all common sense, and the devil now grinned with the power of knowing that his poker face was unnecessary. His hatred was carried out any way possible, depending on the community. It scorned my family relentlessly, daily, and widened the distrust between blacks and whites. This underlined hatred for our people could come in the form of sarcastic laughter, outright insults, or separate eating, drinking, and restroom arrangements.

Every Missouri community seemed to have a set of its own local standards. The one consistent was that it constantly antagonized black families. There was no rest. It could come in the form of a restaurant owner matter-of-factly announcing, "We don't serve your kind here", or it could be as blatant as a sign reading "No niggers allowed". Every racist individual had their own preferences on expressing and utilizing their sickness, and the black communities had to adjust.

And, of course, not every person was racist. Some whites I ran into were downright loving, or at least they thought they were. A few of the nicer white folks might say "hello" or just smile. Other whites might angrily quip, "What you lookin' at, nigger?" But most said nothing, nothing at all. They didn't look at me. They just ignored me completely.

2

"Freedom, but Not Free"

Most every black American lost their true identity when they were stolen, chained, and forced into the Americas as slaves. Most of our people assumed we were African after a couple of generations and just left it as that. We were not simply African! Our identities were stolen along with our bodies. It would take our family, as well as most of our race of people, many decades and a few lines of ancestry to discover who we really are.

Though we became "physically free" around 1865, we were in a specific state of spiritual and mental bondage. White slave owners changed our names and our language. They took away our self-esteem and our sense of worth. They inherited to us a new culture and a different land. Therefore, we were given unsure footing in the lowliest of positions.

We used to sing old Israelite songs. We were the same people who were slaves in Egypt that came out with Moses.

When slavery ended, a justified kind of evil began. In bondage, as long as black folks were in their proper place of work, limited comfort, and in a position to be conveniently punished if need be, everything was fine for whites. Many people smiled as we worked... They patted our kids on the head and went on with their business. But as soon as we be made free? Oh, we were now an irritation that reminded many white folks back then, at least in my mind, that there was no one truly beneath them. And we Negroes were now a threat. A threat to become the great "overcomers" that we are today? No...

no one had foreseen that potential as of yet. But we were now a threat to live a life outside of the slave masters and "overseers'" control, and many an insecure white man was an "overseer". It wasn't enough for us to be poor, tired, hungry, and sad. Many folks had to "see us" as totally hopeless. The legality of the systematic dimensions of slavery kept us where we could be "displayed". Everyone knew where to find us in order to feed those demons of dominance. Those demons existed as an integral part of white nationalism, as natural as breathing. The whites, too, were victims of their own deceptive brainwashing. Did law enforcement care? No, they, too, lived with the same demons. Many of those in charge of governing the lands had no problems with witnessing and accepting illegal activity in the violence against Negroes. This craft of bias fed a far higher hunger than a livelihood based on equality.

You can talk about the Wild West and frontier justice, and that's what it all was back then. A man did what he thought in his heart to do against my people with very little chance of facing any legal implications. In fact, legal consequences of violence against blacks were nonexistent in most parts. We took everything for what we saw at the time... For example, Abraham Lincoln, many blacks thought, was a good and fair man. But we later found out that some of our nation's leaders had ulterior motives, such as financial and political motivations, for the "equality" and the freedom of slaves.

Only God knows the real motives in a man.

Many in the North were jealous and fearful of the southern aristocrats that made so much money off slaves; they felt they had to stop the unfair advantage of a wealth that was being generated from free labor. The massiveness of past slavery is hard to describe. Two-thirds of the South either had slaves or were slaves, and the other third, though not all slave owners, had many of their livelihoods in the services that accompanied slavery... guns, whips, fences, lumber, plows, horses, and anything that assisted in the various kinds of agriculture.

When the slaves were legally freed, there was always the knowledge that this wasn't solely a gesture from moral convictions, it was also political. The black race mostly all joined the new Republican party just because it was the parting from the old evils we knew about in politics. It was the Democratic party who didn't want blacks to vote. It was some of those Democrats who started the KKK. It was many Democrats who thought the black man and woman were inferior. Policing Negroes was an extension of the slave codes that now took root in our law enforcement. Post-slavery mentalities surfaced such as "keep an eye on 'em", "don't trust 'em", "don't let 'em have too much power", and, of course, "a black man can never testify damaging, or even believable, allegations against a white man". Many a county used every scheme they could think of to keep blacks from voting or having an equal voice in American jurisprudence. And, it seemed, that violence and intimidation were their favorite methods of choice.

Intimidation always came first. If intimidation failed to miss its mark for the appropriate control intended, violence quickly followed. It was a common practice, without any formal training, for black folks to engage in postures of inferiority, such as no eye contact, or a quick bow followed by "yes, sir", "no, sir", "yes, ma'am", "no, ma'am". If a confrontation escalated, an exaggerated attitude of being petrified, real or not, would follow. These were the survival tactics of the South and the tip of the Northern States. In the Midwest, that intimidation and aggressiveness was only displayed on some occasions or by some individuals; so blacks and whites communicated much more informally and humanely, just so long as we stayed in our place. Missouri was a strange area for black folks where one had to be flexible either way. We had white folks who insisted on love and equality, and we had those who drank, hated, and "had a rope always ready". Our survival dance had to be as extreme, either way, as the Missouri weather.

The Emancipation Proclamation was "words on paper" that had no impact when horsemen in white hoods came to kill. There were few who enforced the law. The men in blue had marched back North in victory. But the men who had worn gray were even more dangerous than before, because now they were injured animals. And their bite was hard. Bitter, defeated, angry men opened up whole new corridors for demonic infiltration that often came in the form of soothing, therapeutic violence.

Missouri was a state divided like most of the nation. Don't get me wrong, black folks were not the only victims. There were many good white folks strewn throughout the land, and their visions of equality and freedom were also dashed. They suffered a moral and unrighteous sense of loss right along with us. But don't take this wrong either, that, as dejected as they were, except for those in the war, the white folks' worst fears were sadness and poverty, while the black folks constantly had their lives on the line. There were a few cases I heard where a white man was hung right next to the black man that he tried to defend. If his family was harassed for protecting a black family, and he fought and lost, they could all be viciously murdered. But, mostly, for a fair white man, his actions meant moral torment. It was still the same demoralization but on two vastly different planes of reality. Nevertheless, the result of it all was a land divided on many, many levels.

I will never apologize for being black. I will never apologize for how the good Lord made me. I will never give in to the irrational foolishness of people. "Can the Ethiopian change his skin, or the leopard its spots?" Jeremiah 13:23 asks. Today proud black folks might ask, "Why would the Ethiopian ever want to change his skin?" And I would agree wholeheartedly. The emphasis placed on skin color has long lost its intended deception in many today. But it seems that the simple trait of my skin's blackness has led me down this road where many things that impacted my life were because of just that; the fact that my skin just happened to be darker than most people preferred it to be. I never asked to be propelled down involuntary paths exclusively due to my skin color; that was the idea of others. I just hope and pray that most folks don't experience how prejudice can ruin the only life they have. I pray, much more importantly, that the sickness of bigotry can be exterminated before it destroys the souls of many more than the millions it's already destroyed eternally... yes, eternally...

My story reflects both the good and the evil individuals that formed the attitude of our country. My family migrated from the South, in and around Kentucky, to Northwest Missouri, in a town named Cameron, where we got used to being called "darkies". This part of the country had the odd mixture of "northern progressives" and "southern sympathizers". An example of the latter was the infamous Jesse James, born in Kearney, Missouri and shot dead by one of his own men just a few miles away in Saint Joseph. Jesse and his gang lived a life of robbing banks and trains, and even murdered when convenient. And yet their gross rebellion of anything lawful was thought to be heroic by many of the same mindset who lived vicariously through them by reading their heightened tales in newspapers and even adventure books. The double standard of society was and still is apparent. A black man who kills the "non-innocent" to save the lives of his family is a public enemy. A white man who kills the innocent only to scratch a narcissistic itch is eulogized as a hero by top community members, who wink and smile at the violent antics of a spoiled child. Though many knew of his crimes and whereabouts, Jesse was as free as a lark up to the day he was shot in the back and in his own home. Jesse is still celebrated today in annual parades and festivals.

We live in a strange land...

My daddy's grandpa, George Hall, was seven-years-old when the slaves were freed in Kentucky. It was at that time that his family decided to migrate north to move further away from the memories of hatred. Bitterness was in the air as thick as oxygen, and it was "open season on targeting the coloreds".

Down in Kentucky is where my family first found that we had a special gift. Angels would come and visit us. Sometimes these angels would bring visions, sometimes dreams... sometimes they would just talk with us... sometimes they would just sit with us or stand by us. Accurate visions often came into sight for us. We could see the visions playing out like normal people could while watching dramas on a television. At times, someone in my family would know the future or even see a death happening far away while it actually occurred. Some of my family seemed to embrace these visions as a gift, while others seem to see these gifts as depressing and dark... a curse... dreading the involuntary torments that accompanied a knowledge not wanted... and yet amazed at the accuracy of the spiritual discernment, even if the end was tragic. Either way, the spiritual world with its Life and death, Good and evil, Light and overwhelming darkness, clung to my family wherever they roamed, like bark on a tree. It was ingrained in our genetic makeup. Wanted or not, these spiritual gifts were who we were.

Sometimes we heard things from spirits near or far, sometimes we saw things, but our senses were continually open to the spirit realm whenever, wherever, and however the Maker saw fit.

Why do certain people discern the spiritual realm of angels and demons? I don't know, but we have been accused of lying. We have been accused of being witches. We have even been accused of having an overactive imagination or a mental illness. One of my relatives was even put into the insane asylum because of these gifts. These voices, these sightings, are more real than reality itself. I came to know, later in life, that God Himself will show up in the lives of the tormented to let them know that He is still with them. Let there be no mistake, God's Hand rests upon His People. I believe He gives them extra, a very portion of Himself, for their insight and duration to sustain them... a gift always meant for victory, never for evil, and never, ever for quitters.

And so, this was the climate and conditions of the country and the family that I was soon to be born into. I've learned to thank my God for the bad as well as the good. A stage devoid of evil can have no scenes for overcoming. There always got to be the rain if you want to see the flowers... America is a mixed cast of characters, and we write our own scripts.

3

"Here I Am, World"

"**P**ush harder, Sarina, we're almost there," my daddy whispered loudly. "Push harder and don't give up! It's a girl. Isn't she beautiful!"

I was born beside a stillborn twin, and it was originally thought that I, too, would die.

On day one, I was bound for the flesh-filled trash heap of those dead or of no value. This way, the way of the stillborn, would just be a shortcut to an obvious end, without the pain and plagues that occupied the extended version. In the dictionary, the word "stillborn" has two definitions; dead at birth, and useless or ineffectual from the start. As far as society was concerned, we, the two babies, and both black, were both created to fit each definition. I was just the latter...

It was July 19th, 1933, when the doctor picked me up, a baby dead from her mama's womb. In those days, in my hometown Cameron, the doctor was a local white man who came directly into your house for the birth. Whack! He slapped me on the backside... nothing. He turned me over and looked carefully at a faceless child. He removed the "veil" from my face, cleared out my throat, turned me over, and, with a slight shake of his head, he slapped again, holding his large hand down on my tiny buttocks for a moment... Whack! Life!! I struggled to breathe. It was a natural reflex, this yearning to live. My small body was victorious, gasping for air, unaware that my twin had already been set to the side for the baby morgue. Had I known what life was to offer me, I'm quite certain that I would not have minded joining my sibling in the unconscious comfort of death with a quick blink into heaven. But the Lord had other plans for me...

My name is Betty Jackson. And the devil's been trying to silence me since the day I was born. It was that day, I was stillborn with my dead twin. I also had a layer of loose skin and mucous covering my face that the old-timers called a "veil". I prefer to symbolically view this veil in the same terms the Jewish use a veil for their brides in the marriage ceremony. It is their custom that a veil completely hides the face so that all the beauty and purity of the bride is reserved for only the groom. The moment the Jewish bride's face is covered, she is no longer considered single, and no one can look upon what has become the special treasure of her soon-to-be husband. Inside that veil, she belongs to him and him only... Inside my veil I know now I was being held to tell the world how discrimination hurts the very reality of one's view of many, many peoples around the world. For a reason known only by God, on that very first day of my life, He had seen me and preserved me beneath the veil. Death was allowed to only take one of us. It was that day that I came out the lucky one, or unlucky one, depending on how this story hits you.

The veil had been involuntarily removed by a third party. Now I belonged to the world of injustice and not only to God. I would later decisively give myself back to Him. And now I will tell the world what His words of peace are.

My mom, knowing that on the day I arrived in this world there would be no celebration welcoming a newborn for a black woman birthing her first baby girl, she hesitated to get too excited.

"Thank you, God, for this day of celebration," she whispered as she lay her head close to my daddy's cheek. A drop of sweat fastened itself to a tear sliding down the right side of Mama's face... and onto the clean, white surface of the pillow. She prayed, "And, although we walk through the valley of the shadows of death, we bless You, knowing that this is... a... joyous... event."

A black birth in America was considered a natural occurrence... a common cause spoken from a Higher Power, true... but a celebration? A black birth, for obvious reasons during this time period, was not a totally joyous occasion. Although a joyous event, I was an additional expenditure in a family already bound by poverty. I was black in a country that counterfeited equal opportunity. And, if all this wasn't enough, I was born with unique, spiritual gifts given in a culture dominated by charlatans.

No one yet understood my purpose. No one yet knew the horrific destiny life had rolled out for me like a red carpet waiting for the spotlight of my future.

There's an old wives' tale that says: you can see things if you were born with a veil over your face. All I know is that I saw things all the time; things other people didn't see. Angels, visions, dreams... As I grew older, I learned to be very selective who I shared these "sightings" with. Many kids would mock what I saw. Some adults would give me a look like I should be in a loony bin. Either way, I learned to be more careful. In addition, these sightings were a glimpse into the spiritual realm, and it just didn't seem practical to share them with just anyone who lacked the "appreciation" that should accompany the sacred. Besides, I found a thin line between "those the world thought was crazy" versus God's "gifted". I later found a host of exceptional people created by God that people sometimes categorize as "unknowing" or "missing"; special and amazing folks with developmental and cognitive disabilities that were touched by God to be actual geniuses in this world. Ones with superhuman talents and the most rarest of abilities. These wonderful beings should be heard and valued, but we can't see past our cries for survival, the deafening growls from our governing stomachs. Most of all, we can't see past our arrogant cries that demand the way we think all should be...

My vision from time to time was a woman with no face carrying a baby. I don't know for sure who that woman was. I only know that this vision was repeated in my life over and over. And I could hear things, too. At times I would hear music from the air, the most beautiful orchestra I ever heard mixed with the most perfectly harmonized voices from an invisible choir. I somehow knew that it was the angels themselves, but I would hear them as I walked through the woods down the dirt road to our home. I would hear the violins start their indescribable melody, rising over the dusty roads. "Wonderful, Glorious... Omnipotent, Perfect..."

The rocks seemed to shout as I bounced over the river with joy. I would sing, "He alone is our defense. He is worthy of our praise. He will help in time of need..." As I entered into town, I saw townsfolk looking curiously at me. They must have thought I was lacking in my reasoning capacities, as they watched me lift my hands and eyes to God, skipping along and smiling. Sometimes I would stop or slow down when I saw the white folks frowning and shaking their heads. But, other times, the music was just too powerful, too glorious. My heart would continue to praise as if they weren't even there. The angels' anthems sometimes just seemed so much more powerful than the material world around me... a world full of anguish. I would keep right on harmonizing, as I bounced down the middle of the dirt road in my own little world...

My heart would soar beyond all circumstances that surrounded me. It was during these times that my strength felt supernatural!! I could run like a sprinter and not get tired. I felt like I could push up against a brick wall, and it would move gracefully. I don't know why God chose me and my family to carry these perceptions into the world. But I do know this... There are those who can grasp truth solely because they can dream it; and there are those who can grasp the spiritual realm, for the simple reason that they see it every day.

4

"WitchCraft"

Before I was born, there was a black woman who promised my mom a layette of clothes if she named me Josephine. A few days later, the woman brought by the briefcase and, again, promised to fill the entire bag with "hand-me-downs" if my mom went ahead and named me after her. So my mother named me Josephine Elizabeth Jackson in agreement with the woman's promise. But I guess I wasn't what the woman thought I should be. After she heard I was born, she came by for a visit, picked me up, and looked at me (so the story goes), set me back down, borrowed the briefcase back, and never returned. It was then that my mom nicknamed me Betty.

Another day, I watched In the front yard as my mother sat humming a praise song while sewing a sleeve from a torn shirt in the front yard. A fire under a pot of boiling clothes crackled, steaming in front of her. She had laundry hanging to her right and a basket of clothes to her left. Another fire was burning inside with a large pot of some kind of soup going... She rocked in her chair, sang, and hummed. "Lord, I know that you are over all," she muttered between hymns. "I place You over me. I die to myself and ask you to live inside me instead... I need you, Father."

Just then, one of her young sons ran by and aggressively pulled his sisters' hair. Mom picked up the stick from the boiling laundry pot, put her sewing packet down, gave a perfect slap on his buttocks, while all at the same time utterly correcting the lad with a stare!

Afterwards, she went inside and stirred the pot of soup, went back outside and stirred the clothes, sat back down and commenced to sewing again, as if nothing happened. "Thank you, Lord," she muttered, and then went back to humming. All day long my mom could balance five or six tasks at once. Laziness was not a luxury or convenience back then. If a parent got the chance to soak in the tub or the nearby pond for twenty minutes, that was a welcome "spoiling" from the Maker.

On another note: My mom's daddy was John Tapp. He couldn't read or write, but he had a very literate talent for being able to count money. No one could fool John Tapp when it came to counting money or keeping track of money. His other talent was being able to play the fiddle. He played the fiddle by ear without needing printed music, lessons, or backup. He would play the fiddle for all the square dances and other celebrations around town.

John Tapp was the first one I heard of in our family who had the "gift".

One day, big John Tapp was chopping up wood for a certain white man named Nelson. While he was working, he noticed that Mr. Nelson had disappeared and hadn't come back for a while. When hiring one of us, Mr. Nelson always made it his business to keep an eye on the black folks he hired. He usually watched Mr. Tapp and conversed with him whenever John worked for him.

After a while, John became concerned. He walked onto the front porch and peered inside the door screen.

"Mr. Nelson," John called out. But no answer. "Mr. Nelson, you okay?" John shouted, as he knocked on the door. "Hmm, where you at, Mr. Nelson?" John muttered. He walked around each side of the house, peeked inside the back window, and there he saw Mr. Nelson's boots. His legs were stretched across the floor. John ran around the front door and entered. Mr. Nelson had died right there on the floor while John was outside working.

But John was not a man who squabbled about small details. After making sure that Mr. Nelson was truly dead, John went back outside and kept on chopping wood. After all, Mr. Nelson had already paid him when he arrived. There was no ambulance and no 911 calls. When a man died, he was dead. Mr. Nelson had no family and lived so far out that no one really spoke much to him. John walked all the way into town, after the wood was completely hewed, and told the sheriff that Mr. Nelson was lying dead on the floor. All the locals knew and trusted John, so that was that.

"Well, boy..." the sheriff drawled, while continuing his paperwork. "With John being the last of his relatives around here, I guess you'd better go on back out there and bury him." John stared at the sheriff for a few seconds, until the sheriff finally looked up at him. "Well, okay, then," John said, double-checking the sheriff's expression to make sure it was okay to leave. "I'll go on back out there and do that."

John walked all the way back out to Mr. Nelson's house, dragged the cold body out to the side yard where the ground was softer, and began digging. He dug a nice, deep hole about four-feet deep, rolled Mr. Nelson in, and shoveled the dirt on top of him. Then John went back out front where the wood was chopped, and stacked it all up neatly to complete the job.

"There... " he said. "Mr. Nelson, things are gonna' be alright now."

After this, John sat down against the tree for a rest and fell into a deep sleep. John began to dream. Mr. Nelson walked up to him in the dream and looked at him while he slept. Then he went over and surveyed the huge stack of neatly cut wood. Mr. Nelson turned back to John. "I came back for my wood," he said in the dream to John.

"But I done buried you, Mr. Nelson," John replied in the dream.

About an hour later, John woke out of his sleep. When he looked over, all the wood was gone. He looked back at the fresh grave. The dirt was still on top of Mr. Nelson. All John knew is that the spirit ghost of Mr. Nelson had wanted the wood, and now it was gone.

To my family, it was just "one of them things." When John told the story, or whenever another unexplained occurrence happened between the spirit realm and that of the physical, it didn't need to make sense. After all, none of the world around us made sense. Slavery, prejudice, hate-filled looks.... What use then would a stack of wood be for a dead man? Awww... It didn't matter, nor did they try to decipher the logic of it. Longing for its relevance, they would always tell the story, shake their heads, and then move on without much more insight than, "It was just one of them things... It sure was... Uh, huh..." Then they would secretly embrace for whatever blessing God had in store to show them next.

My mom's daddy, Big John Tapp, must have handed "the gift" down to Daddy. He could also see things, amazing things, vividly in the clouds. The clouds served as his tapestry. And we weren't so sure if he saw the natural formation of a cloud that was affecting the eyes of the human spirit, or if the clouds themselves spiritually fashioned what Daddy was seeing in his head. But what we understood is that Daddy rarely missed the opportunity to express that the cloud formations were a message from God of what God wanted to show him, and he always appreciated the sight.

One day, we lay down in the grass on a hillside. "You see that?" Daddy asked, pointing at a massive cloud. "That there is Abraham Lincoln." It was absolutely uncanny. I saw, as clear as can be, the clouds perfectly forming a man sitting at a desk in the sky. It was so clear! I could even see how Mr. Lincoln was dressed in a handsome suit. I couldn't believe it...

We strolled up and down the paths of the rolling country hills. "Well, would you look at that," Daddy stopped and said. He squatted down and squinted at another masterpiece in the sky. Holding his chin, he said. "Wow, Betty.... quell splendor!"

The sky provided Daddy with glorious artwork all day long. We never needed galleries, museums, or art fairs. We couldn't afford to go to art galleries, expositions, and such, like the white children around us. Black families were not allowed to participate in these things, so God filled in our lack of experiencing those marvels with greater forms of entertainment. God gave us more than what the wealthiest of men could go to or witness on the earth. They had their tuxedos, top hats, and fancy cars taking them to giant stone buildings that held the most renowned expressions of art from all over the world. Daddy merely had to look at the colors in the sky that bypassed anything man could imagine. The artwork of angels emerged, it seemed, whenever Daddy looked up to the heavens with the most trusted expectations.

It was simply His caress on the dispossessed.

Grandpa John Tapp's wife was Grandma Lula. She would walk a long way to church while singing the hymn, "By and by when the morning come. All the saints of God goes gathering home. We will tell the stories of how we overcome, and we will understand it better by and by..."

"We are tossed and driven on the restless sea of time," her voice rose up with the dawning light of a fresh Sunday morning. "Somber skies and howling tempests oft succeed a bright sunshine. In that land of perfect day, when the mists are rolled away, we will understand it better by and by..."

Even the birds stopped and listened! Tweeting along, so it seemed... "By and by, when the morning comes, when the saints of

God are gathered home... They will tell the story how they've overcome and will understand it better by and by!"

Grandma Lula often quickened the pace, raising her right hand to heaven, while holding her large, yellow hat with her left hand. "We are often destitute of the things that life demands," she wailed. "Want of food and want of shelter, thirsty hills and barren lands. We are trusting in the Lord."

That evening, Grandpa John Tapp lay comfortably in his bed before going to sleep.

"The Master will be after me tonight," big John spoke, closing his eyes.

It was a bit early to sleep as the sun outside had barely disappeared behind the distant hills. Family members and close friends came in and out, as they normally did on Sunday evenings. Of course they usually greeted Lula first, the lady of the house, and then went into the pantry to grab something that was always set aside for hungry guests to eat. Everyone ate, prayed, laughed, argued... all the while listening to John in his bedroom cry out against the wall repeating, "The Master will be after me tonight..."

Once in a while, someone would ask, "What's John talkin' 'bout?" But mainly the same festivities continued. Just like any other Sunday evening, small groups or individuals came through the front door grabbing a plate, filling it up, and then sitting on the porch to converse. Usually they spoke about the Lord, but there was always some juicy family gossip mixed in there, too… and lots and lots of laughter.

But tonight, through it all, John kept his eyes closed and continued muttering, "The Master will be after me tonight."

After everyone went home and the candles were blown out, quick bursts of lightning sizzled throughout the sky. Somewhere far away, rolls of thunder interrupted a nearby coyote's yells... along with the death songs of crickets.

Some time that night, Grandpa John died in his sleep. The Master had come and swept him away without disturbing anyone.

5

"Family"

I was born the third eldest of twelve. First, there was a baby girl, Margaret Ellen. She died when she was only five-days-old. Second came George. If you spent any time at all with George, the first thing you noticed was his intelligence. He could observe the world and make quips about it like no one I ever heard. "Look at the new group of bees that showed up this week," George spoke one day. He always used a clear and proper English dialect. Just then, he would quickly write something down on a notepad he carried around.

"Those are the Western honeybees that commonly live an average of one to ten months." He spoke on. "They are distinctly different from the Leafcutters and Mason bees. They're from the same family as the Carpenter bees from the family Apidae. Now, Carpenter bees have stingers that are not barbed, and so they can sting you over and over again..."

George jumped up on a wooden fence overlooking a small field. "Their pollinating patterns differ from the common bumblebee. They play a crucial role in the foods we eat."

At times, someone would respond to George, and even try to carry on a conversation. But, sooner or later, everyone was much too busy to stay and listen to George's ongoing dialogue about things that only George himself seemed interested in. "And, unlike bumblebee colonies, honeybee colonies are meant to thrive year after year with thousands of bees..."

On this particular rant, I made the mistake of correcting George at that point by asking, "Why would a colony thrive year after year if they only live one to ten months?" George looked at me patiently and pushed his glasses up on his nose before going into a long explanation of scientific rhetoric that I didn't want to listen to.

But, I must admit, George could observe the often-overlooked things of the world and make speeches about them like I never heard before. I had no doubt that George would be some sort of professor. He also had a gift for the literary world. He would read book after book. And he had the most beautiful handwriting I'd ever seen!

Unfortunately, George's greatness was never realized by anyone outside the family. George had his body attacked and crippled by rickets so that it was hard for him to move like a healthy, young man. He still had his wonderful mind, though, until a certain event occurred. Later, I realized that George was comparing the bees to the various kind of white folks he was around in those days. George's observations were always deeper than they seemed on the surface. He also dug and sold worms to the local fishermen.

One day, Daddy, Mamma, and I saw George out back crawling around on his hands and knees like a baby. He had a big knot on his head and his glasses were broken.

"What's wrong, George?" each of us asked, one after another.

But all he did was rub his head, delicately re-push his broken glasses upon his nose, and then stare down at the ground again. Finally he answered, "A horse kicked me."

I halfway expected George to say much, much more about the horse family, the evolution of horses, their migrating patterns based on grazing cycles, and reasons or defense mechanisms that might result in the act of kicking... But that was all George said. No one witnessed or knew what really happened or how it happened. So I assume that George knew what he was talking about. Those were the last clear words I ever heard from the mouth of George.

The sharp-witted, intellectual young man, with the perfect handwriting, was like a baby for many years. He lost his speech and would just babble. I believe his sharp mind worked, but he stared at us like a man trapped within himself. His eyes seemingly begged for someone to rescue him out of that tortured shell of a body. His mind just didn't cooperate to get the words out. His body seemed paralyzed at times, and, after a while, everyone just seemed to run around him like he was a piece of furniture.

Then there was me, Betty.

I grew up, as many children do within a large family. Not realizing we were poor and being naive of the significance of my skin color, I stayed innocent. Not counting the twin that died by my side, I became fully aware that there were the same number of kids in our family as the twelve tribes of Israel. And, though my complexion and my poverty hadn't hit my conscious state of reality, it didn't take long for "the capability"... my electromagnetism with the spiritual realm, that started its unique call.

I was just a young girl when my grandmother died. Over time, I watched curiously as Grandma Lula would start talking to some invisible person while rocking in her chair. She began to pay less attention to the people and things around her and began to give more attention to an invisible reality of a Being or beings that we couldn't see or hear as she could. Finally, as she rocked closer towards her bed one night, I just knew, somehow, that once asleep, she was not going to wake up. However, I kept the secret to myself and decided to observe.

I crept in the shadows and studied her deep breathing, as she lay down quietly after entering her bed. She wasn't in any pain. She just closed her eyes and breathed like a young child. And then I saw them for the first time in my life; strange, bright lights all around her, moving rhythmically, almost dancing, as she continued to inhale and exhale her last breaths. The lights surrounded her body, evenly spaced, dancing... Seemingly enjoying their special assignment, I was awestruck. I knew, deep in my soul, instinctively, that these lights were angels. I wasn't scared. These beautiful, dancing lights soothed me beyond all thoughts of fear or anything that death would reveal. A calm empowerment came over me. I comprehended their purpose and their dance. These angels were waiting patiently, obediently in celebratory movements to usher my grandmother into heaven the moment she passed.

Grandma Lula had been faithful and obedient to Jesus. And now, as her frail body was surrendering its limited authority, my grandmother was seconds away from being more free than she'd ever been. Ushered out of this dark world full of color-filled hatred, I was humbled and honored to be there, witnessing the whole majestic scene. Angels... the hidden, powerful servants of the Most High God who so many folks consider symbolic or mythological... but then they uncovered themselves in full view. There they were "brown" angels dancing in my house! White wings with brown bodies! All the pictures I'd ever seen of angels were white. Wow! What a relief to know that angels of color were here to take her home. They seemed to move closer to grandmother, and her face seemed to glow.

"Grandma!" I exhaled breathlessly.

"Home," she whispered turning back toward the bouncing lights and other angels. "Home," she said.

I knew then that Grandma had been waiting for the angels, too. Calm as could be, she repeated slowly, yet with strength and power, "I'm... goin'... home."

Then Grandma pointed towards the sky. Finally her arm fell as she breathed her last breath out ever so slowly, resting her hand next to her side. Grandma Lula had made it to her "By and by", and the lights, other angels, and their dancing disappeared.

I sat there for a long time in silence with the feeling that I was now alone. The glowing lights had left with Grandma's soul. Grandma would never be back. Gone for eternity... eternity... eternity... that word stirred more in my soul than my mind. Grandma had described eternity to me one day, after I had asked, "How can something never end? It's got to end someday, don't it?"

"Eternity's like a constant-moving circle," she had said one evening, watching the sunset.

It took me a while to realize that my family was different from most, even in how they died. At one time, I just figured that all folks saw spirits. But as I got older and began to talk to those outside of my family, I noticed the strange looks they gave me as I explained one family member passing after another. Being fairly sensitive, I also noticed their desire to avoid me later.

I then again began to fully remind myself that our informal conversations about spirits, ghosts, etc... were generational and, therefore, very strange to most folks outside of family. It became commonplace in our home to hear story after story each week, while sitting around the fire kennel or out on the front porch.

From listening to those stories, I came to deduce certain similarities that were common among our sightings. Angels were among the most recurring. Few things on earth are more brilliant than an angel waiting in a "guarded position". I'm not talking now about the bouncing lights; I'm speaking of real angels that I saw in their physical forms. These angels, their "armor" extraordinary and their figures shining with unmatched beauty, ranged from smaller than five-feet-tall to several hundred-feet-tall. Most of the time, the angels acted completely unaware that we were watching them conducting their business. At times, another angel of God, seemed to flow indiscreetly, with indescribable elegance, in a most business-like fashion. Their very movements were intimidating, yet graceful, powerful… royal. Their distinctive style were so intense and yet calm. I would hate to ever have one of them mad at me.

Then, also, we would see the powers of Satan's army. They, on the other hand, were just the opposite. A cloud of pure darkness accompanied their presence. Some of them came in the form of white bats with torn wings flying through the atmosphere. Physically, I only know to describe them as pure ugly… beyond hideous. There really are no words to describe them. Just pure evil. Evil that sometimes takes on their form through the hearts of men. I hope that humans will understand that if they have hate in their heart toward any man because of the color of their skin, that the evil one has taken its root inside the heart and has made a home in the temple of your body. After death, it will not be good for that individual…

Our Hollywood adaptations of demons, devils, and the underworld are not even close in fashioning an accurate portrayal. Their physical make-up with their movements are designed to strike fear and terror into anyone who dares to oppose them. If people could see only the sheer hatred in their eyes as they target their intended, usually oblivious, victims… well, let's just say people who are not concerned with what is happening around them, or the individuals who just simply choose to hate with no real reason… They would run, literally run, to repentance at the sight of the demonic!

Devils hate us beyond normal, human understanding, because we are made in the image of God, along with the love He feels for us. People who hate people without real cause, will experience an eternal division away from God's presence and protection. Destruction after death awaits them as an eternal enemy. Like a reflection of their own inner soul…

If someone feels suddenly bad or depressed for no logical reason, it's because a spirit of darkness has come to rest in their immediate proximity or actually upon the spirit body. Their wicked presence can grab your very soul, your inner being that no one can see, and drag it down into a hopeless, cruel pit of pure gloom. Their top deception is that they might make one believe they don't exist at all. That way, the demons' "hidden" effects can "trick" men. They can trick a man to become dependent on alcohol, drugs, medicines, sex, or anything else that helps him to stop thinking about hopelessness. They can trick a man to mistreat another man, even to the point of destroying him. They can even make men want to take their own lives, because we are tricked into thinking that it's our own inner being, or our own consciousness that is dark and consumes hopelessness. With no belief that these unpleasant beings exist, a man is left to betray only himself. And that is the greatest lie of all. Hating another man because he's different from yourself betrays one's self.

Most men will live their entire lives believing the spirit realm to be mythological, and yet we feel their draining effects on our lives every single day. What we consider an emotional, generational, scientific spectrum of biological moodiness or gleefulness, could easily have been coerced by an angel on assignment. These are actual beings living and affecting our world and our destinies in a spiritual world that is much more real than understood. The consequences on how we respond will have extreme implications on ourselves and the world around us.

I'm convinced, as I watch men and women of every color and circumstance, that we are born with an undiluted, natural evil that these spirits bring. Only the salvation of our Lord Yeshua changes our course if we pray and trust in Him.

So the stories we would tell in "public", on our porches, in our yards, and outside our homes, were more associated with human event experiences of supernatural activities.

"You know I saw ol' Jonesy up at the store," my daddy would say. "He told his friend that I was the nicest darky he knew."

"I didn't know Jonesy was like that," Mama would chime in. "Callin' us darkies..."

Lots of people in Missouri referred to us as darkies. If a white lady asked another white lady, "Oh, whose little girl is this?" The answer might be something to the liking of, "Oh, this precious, little darky belongs to the family down by the park." Some folks said it really nice and polite, completely unaware of its racist content. Some said it rather mean, being fully aware of its offensiveness. And then some just said it with a slight smirk and looked for your reaction.

"The preacher called me a darky on Sunday," my cousin said, chewing on a mouthful of food and sitting down with a freshly-packed plate. "He said, 'Somebody find this darky a bible, if he can read'... He was really nice."

"That ain't nice," a voice yelled out from the kitchen. "That preacher got some nerve..."

"Could you see one of our elders saying, 'Get this whitey a bible'?" a voice yelled out.

"Hell, nah," several said.

"My teacher said that I was a darky with spunk!" a child's voice echoed though the noise.

"Better be careful," my cousin laughed. "Last nigga' with spunk I saw was hangin' from a tree!"

Many times these conversations would carry on heavily into the evening hours. The laughing, crying, the emotional outbursts of pain, served its purpose of just trying to make it through the night hoping for better days ahead.

How amazing that men actually believe that we are different because of skin color. That has to be one of the greatest falsehoods of all time. I sometimes wonder how many white folks the devil's heart took simply for despising black people... And then, how many black folks the devil's heart influenced by having them hate one another?

And then I marveled at why people called us darkies. I knew that it was from the demonic- filled realm I once experienced from these kind of individuals. Darkness referred often to evil; or it could refer to someone not having clarity. But to attach these negative perceptions to us as a people? How ironic, to me, that the ones with the lighter complexions that were throwing out the term were much more apt to have the dual nature of the darkness.

And yet they called us darkies...

I told my friend Becky this. She told her mom, and her mom told her to stay away from me. It seemed to me that some of us "darkies" had much more "enlightenment" towards the truths of the spiritual realm. Whether we're talking about a black woman dancing in the fields under the anointing of the Holy Spirit, or a black man casting voodoo spells under the influence of witchcraft, it seemed that people of color were much more in touch with the spiritual realm, or at least it felt so back then. I often wondered why the discrepancy was so vast between colors.

I used to think that perhaps it was because there had always been generally less material wealth to blind the people of color. Perhaps the good Lord placed greater perception inside black folks as a way of evening out the cruel disadvantages they felt from society.

But one Sunday, I was in church. Back then, in every church in Cameron, there were only white preachers.

This day I looked around at my surroundings with deep focus, a concentration from the Spirit. I looked at the white people nodding in the front. I looked at the black folks that were made to sit in the balcony, heads bowed. I always found a chair on the side where I could spot the whole church and sit unnoticed, and the white ushers never seemed to mind. After all, I was just a child. I opened the hymn book and studied the songs... the authors were white men after white men from England. I looked up at the artwork around the vestibule and sidewalls. The stained-glass images on the windows were beautiful. I searched every sun-reflected color of their stories; a white John the Baptist baptizing a white Jesus; a white Mary holding a white baby next to a white man with a staff; twelve white men around a table with another one in the middle; a white woman kissing the feet of a white man... And then I looked behind the white preacher, who stood and calmly spoke in front of the huge face of a white Jesus.

I fell asleep and awoke to the people standing for a final prayer. After church, the preacher's wife, a blond lady named Glenda, came up to me in her usual, perky way. She patted me on the head and handed me a lollipop.

"Thank you, ma'am," I said.

"Oh, you're welcome," Glenda smiled at me. "We're gonna' eat some food later, but you better run along home before your parents wonder where you are."

"Ma'am?" I hesitated to speak. I legitimately wondered about all the white images I had studied.

She stopped and bent down. She held my hand gently.

"Yes," Glenda answered. "Do you need anything?"

"Um," I stammered slowly, putting the lollipop in my mouth quickly before taking it back out. I pointed at the stained-glass windows.

"Yes," Glenda said excitedly, glancing towards the windows and holding my hand more firmly.

"Um, are there any black people that were in the bible?" I finally blurted out.

Glenda quickly released my hand but kept smiling. She walked towards a portion of the window that partially had a face uncovered at the far corner of the stained-glass window. It looked like a portion of a man's brown face with a big hat on top of his head.

"One of the wise men was black," Glenda said proudly. "He came from a faraway land to see the new baby Jesus and give him gifts! Isn't that exciting?"

I stood there a bit puzzled, wondering why I didn't notice that portion of the window during service.

Glenda came back over to me and bent down again.

"Little girl, you are from Africa," Glenda said smoothly. "You are from a faraway land. But it don't matter what African tribe your people came from... The bible says that your people were pagans. But that's all over now. Paul preached to the pagans and the Gentiles. You can be grafted into us now!"

"I can be what?"

"Grafted in means that you can be tied into the tree..."

"What?" I blurted out while involuntarily taking a step backwards.

"You can be added to the vine and become a part of it," Glenda explained, composing herself, while quickly glancing around to see if anyone heard her. She then looked back down at me with pity trying to find the right words.

"I better go," I finally said. "Thank you for the lollipop."

That night I had a dream. Drums were banging, and violent lightning flashed with a brewing storm, in the night skies over the sands of a desert. Over the hill came a man with a staff walking. He was a stern-faced, brown man with flowing gray hair. And behind him came a line of brown people, men, women, children, tall, short, old, young... a line of people about twenty across, marching like soldiers. And over the hill came line after line of people, all black and different shades of brown. And they kept coming as far as the eye could see, the noise from the drums becoming more intense... I lifted my eyes like the wings of a bird flying over the desert dunes. The people, like ants, poured over hill after hill... I heard the banging from the drums become louder and louder... closer and closer...

On July 19th, 1933, I, Betty Jackson, came into this world. And the supernatural had always walked and talked with our family if we listened and took notice of them. I came to know very early in life that some kind of violent battle was going on in this world... and the angels and demons were much more focused on it than we were. As a matter of fact, that battle, the battle for souls, was their *only* focus. Souls that were willing to follow. Souls that were lost. Wondering souls that grappled at nothing...

I continued to dream, watching in amazement the flowing, brown people coming over the earth's horizon. The number was overwhelming. Their power was magnificent.

An angel came and whispered in my ear. "Betty... Betty..."

I lay there pretending to sleep.

"Betty," the angel whispered. "Your people were not pagans. Your people were not Gentiles. Your people are God's chosen people..."

"What?" I whispered, thinking about the contradiction from what the pastor's wife had said.

"Your People are God's People," the angel whispered.

I could still hear the loud drums. I thought about the many great, proud People, walking in unison, the lightning flashing in the skies above them.

"Betty," the angel whispered again, but I noticed a bit more urgency in his voice as he spoke the words with an alarming type of magnitude. The softness had disappeared and there was a daunting authority to his tone. "Betty... you are from the tribe of Judah!"

I may have been born dead, unwanted, of no value, and left for the trash heap, but an unusual lowliness is often a similar start to many of God's greatest victories!

Life is so amazing at times...

The angel touched my hair as I nodded back to sleep. He smiled. And then he stood up, his armor shining against the rising sun. He adjusted a huge sword with his hand that sat ready on his right hip.

"You are from the tribe of Judah," he said one last time.

I slowly awoke, opening my eyes and listening to the various birds breaking the morning silence... his voice slowly faded away...

6

"Missouri"

Pop! The raggedy baseball comes off my bat as I swing as hard as I can, but it only manages a downward angle to the left about 20 feet. But I'm fast. And, as I make it to first, I see that the fielder is focused on chasing a runner who had taken off from third base. So I dart off to second and make it easily, as the other runner crosses the plate.

"Brian, you're so stupid," a bigger kid yells at the fielder. "How you gonna' let him score and let her go to second?"

"Aw, shut up," a wiry girl named Suzy blurts out, defending her little brother. "I don't see you doing so great. We're hittin' everything you're throwing!"

We had twelve kids playing that day; six on each side. Some of the kids had gloves, but I just played with my bare hands. Ten of the kids are white and two black, but it doesn't matter.

As I look back, what I remember most about my hometown, are the sun-drenched days of running and playing with the white kids. To us kids, there was no skin color. There was how tall you were, how fast you could run, how good of a swimmer you were, how funny you were, how good were the stories you told, and if your parents gave you money for the ice cream truck or not... Now those things made you popular, but color was a non-factor. It just ranked way too far behind other components that mattered more in the minds of each kid.

Suzy was my best friend. She always seemed to defend two things, her little brother and what was right. She was fearless. "You're my best friend, Betty," she told me one day under a shade tree, after an especially long game on an especially hot day. "I love you, and I hope we'll always stay best friends."

"Me, too," I answered, honored that the rough, tough Suzy momentarily ignored her reputation and verbalized a unique, loving part of her that included me.

Life as a child was carefree and fair like baseball. I loved playing baseball. There were rules that nobody thought to break. When it's time for "batter up," you get to hit in your given order, and everybody gets an equal chance. You've got to catch that ball if it's hit to you. You run to bases where you're safe or out! If you clearly get to the bag before they tag you, no one thinks to call you out, no matter who you are. The same rules apply to every participant.

Baseball rules are supreme above the physical attributes or even the athleticism of who's playing. Baseball rules are supreme above how rich you are or how poor you are. Baseball itself doesn't care who wins or loses. Baseball is a game of justice. The game's rules are based on the moral code of what is right and fair. Funny how an unimportant game can be so fair, while our own human significance can be so unequivocally contrary.

Crack! Now the ball is hit just to my right and fielded by the same boy, Brian, who starts tirelessly chasing me. But I'm flying down to third, right past him. And I break out into uncontrollable giggling, easily passing him as he struggles to catch me. Now he's mad! His face turns bright red, irritated by my quickness, as I dip my shoulder and avoid his tag. I easily make it to third, but I'm not stopping. Without breaking stride, I fly towards home plate. Brian stops and throws to the catcher. The ball gets there before I do. But the catcher, in his hurry to get the ball and tag me, fumbles the ball and it drops at his feet while he still tries to tag me with an empty glove.

By now, I'm laughing. "You got to tag me with the ball, idiot," I yell, while tagging home plate.

"You guys all stink!" the older pitcher screams. "How can you let her score?"

I'm laughing so hard that my stomach starts to hurt, as Brian throws his glove down as hard as he can, looking like a red balloon from the shoulders up.

"Way to go, Betty!" Suzy, who's on my team, shrieks as she punches me on my arm. She steps past me with her bat, because she's up next. But also she wants to make sure the older pitcher doesn't yell at her brother again. Eyeballing him as she swings the bat, Brian warily looks towards her, grumbles a few words, and walks back to the mound area.

Some days, we would play baseball three hours, go home, get a fast sandwich, and then everyone would meet at the swimming hole, where a whole new set of games and challenges filled the hot afternoon going into the early evenings. Yes, life was fair and joyful among us kids.

But skin color for my daddy was a much different story. Joshua Jackson had fought bravely in World War I. As a matter of fact, he was also a Buffalo soldier. He had risked his life for a country that treated him far less than an American citizen. He had to sharply answer, "Yes, sir" and "no, sir" in the United States Army to a superior rank. However , after the war, when he came back to Cameron, he had to answer, "Yes, sir" and "no, sir" to farmers, store owners, and other local men who had no military status as civilians, but were equal to him; and many of them who hadn't once served to defend the country. While Daddy ducked bullets on the front lines of a strange country on the other side of the sea, these same men never stopped the comforts of their daily routines; working their jobs, growing their crops, and drinking their moonshine into the night. And how did many of our country men repay the protector of such freedoms? By rudely barking orders at him, humiliating him. To Daddy, it felt like another form of slavery.

"Hey, boy," a white man yelled as Joshua approached the front of a local eatery. "You got to go around the back if you want to eat here..."

"Yes, sir," Joshua turned and said with a slight nod of confusion. "I'm just wantin' to have a word with Mr. Reynolds about plowin' his field."

Mr. Reynolds was standing on the front porch of the restaurant, lighting a cigar while laughing and talking to another man.

"Watch your tone, boy," the man yelled, after Joshua had slightly turned around to approach Mr. Reynolds. Joshua was hoping Mr. Reynolds would notice him, and that way it would make it easier to deal with any overwhelming pride that might cause Mr. Reynolds to overreact in front of the townsmen.

"Mr. Reynolds, you still want me to plow your field this spring?" Joshua asked, keeping his head down and eyes lowered, as he had seen his daddy do so many times, while glancing up strategically every so often.

"I'm in a conversation, Mr. Jackson," Mr. Reynolds said abruptly.

"Yes, sir... sorry, sir... I was just wonderin'..." Joshua stepped back a couple of steps. Again, this was a strategy learned partly from experience and partly from instincts. Joshua thought, *if I act the part, pretending that I might have to go on with my busy day, this Reynolds fellow might realize that he missed out on the cheap labor being offered to him. Then he would have to hire a more expensive white laborer, who will probably do a job of less quality and thoroughness.*

Or, God forbid, he might have to do the job himself. White men in Missouri, who loved to act rich, were usually doing just that... acting. And part of the act was to hire out men to do the work of the land. The black worker offered dual benefits; the black worker gave into the game that the hirer was superior, and he did it at a bargain price.

By far, the black man offered the best deal for the best work. Mr. Reynolds knew that, and Joshua knew that Reynolds knew that. But that didn't stop the two of them from playing this prideful dance...

Joshua took a few more steps backward as if to warn Mr. Reynolds that the offer only stood for a limited time and that he would soon be leaving the premises.

"Well, since you already interrupted me..." he said carefully to Joshua, while puffing his cigar.

"You got your own plow?"

"No, sir," Joshua replied. "I'd be needin' to borrow yours. Mine got stolen while I was overseas... But I got me my own horse."

"Fine, fine," Mr. Reynolds said with a wave of his hand to indicate he was finished speaking.

"We'll talk about the price later."

"Well, if it's all the same to you sir, I'd like to talk price now," Joshua said, while ignoring his raised eyebrow. "... so as to not have to interrupt you again later, sir."

Joshua was extremely intelligent and sly in a secretive way. He knew that a price quote from Mr. Reynolds while in front of another white man would work on Mr. Reynolds' reputation in the community as a "God-fearing", just man, and the price would be much more fair than one quoted later in private. They agreed to the price and time, and Joshua made his exit with a slight smile as he turned towards home.

My daddy was not only intuitive, he could also do just about anything. His mom had died when he was fourteen, so he learned to get along inside the home by cooking and cleaning, and outside of it, by making money. He worked for the white folks doing all the odd jobs that no one else wanted to do; yard work, building, plowing, painting, and cleaning. He had his own modest acre, where he raised hogs and chickens before selling them at the market. We had two horses for plowing our garden and two cows for our milk. Daddy also had a big garden in which he grew many vegetables. We always had enough to eat.

A few days later, as Joshua prepared for his trek home after plowing Mr. Reynolds' field, he suddenly stopped in front of a big pile of wood, brush, metal, and other trash.

Hmm, Daddy said to himself. He continued walking, while leading his horse named Quick behind him.

House by house, acre by acre, he walked past... stopping every once in a while, he stared, as he saw more piles of rubble stacked on properties.

Hmm, he said, deep in thought each time he saw another pile. "How 'bout that, Quick. You see that, Quick?"

Then Joshua stopped and saw something in the clouds. A wide grin formed on his face.

"Thank you, Lord," he whispered, starting to walk home at a faster pace. "C'mon, Quick... giddup... here we go... Thank you, God."

That night, Joshua hung lights outside to work around an old, non-running car that someone had given him. Daddy never turned down junk... he would always find some use for it. This night, Daddy got out his saw and began to work. I woke up several times in the night, looking out my window, and watching Daddy sawing, hammering, and talking to himself. Once in a while, he would start singing a happy song, or I would hear him cussing in the middle of something he could not easily fix!

"Get back to sleep, Betty," Daddy snapped, after seeing my head in the window.

The next morning, Joshua's invention was completed. He had formed a half-car, half-truck, that had a huge, wide bed in the back.

"What's that, Daddy?" I asked, after eating my breakfast and rushing outside.

"This here is my trash hauler," Joshua said cheerfully, relieved he was finished. "I'm gonna' do a service for these people out here by hauling all their stuff away to the dump."

"People will pay for that?" I asked.

"Folks will pay a little, Betty... But a whole lotta' littles adds up to a lot!"

And Daddy did just that. He must have made deals with half the people in the county for bi-weekly pickups. Daddy had tapped into a business need that would provide us with something we had never had before, regular cash flow. Daddy seemed happier, not having to go out and deal with the unpredictability and humiliation of constantly looking for work opportunities every day.

So every morning, Joshua was up running his routes. He perfected his trash hauling schedule to hit different parts of town on different days. He used his ingenuity, not only to make money, but to supplement the provisions that he was already involved in. For example, he would pick out the "reusable garbage" that could feed his pigs. Then he would put certain kinds of garbage in a wheel barrel he had made and then mix and distribute homemade "slop".

Occasionally, my dad would run into the "good trash", such as cinnamon or dinner rolls, mostly found at supermarkets, expired, that the owner had thrown out. Joshua would carefully clean the food, break off the bad parts, and we would have bread or rolls warmed in the oven on our table the next day. No one knew the difference.

My daddy was the most resourceful and intelligent man I knew. If food got low, he would fish at the local ponds or hunt for deer, squirrel, raccoon, or possum. We always had more than enough food. Eggs from chickens, vegetables from the garden, fish, meat, apples and walnuts from Daddy's trees, Mamma's homemade bread... And for the next forty years, my dad hauled trash in and around Cameron, Missouri.

So trash became our family's source of stability. There were some whites who refused to allow my daddy a steady income by denying him the job of holstering their trash weekly, but every white person was not racist against Daddy, of course.

I recall so many wonderful, friendly white people in Northwest Missouri. One man I worked for would invite me in to eat at his own dinner table. Though this was taboo at the time, the man simply said, "If you're good enough to work for me, you're good enough to eat with me." I remember the white parents who would let their kids come over to our house to stay the night. Life in America was a mixed array of good and bad, blessings and curses, for a black family. And, of course, life was always a little easier in the community if you were a black female versus a black male.

Again, my daddy saw another side of it all, being a black man and a rather large one at that. Discrimination seemed to follow him everywhere he went, like a cloud blocking the rays of sunlight. The trains were a huge commodity in our town. Once, we had three train stations, including the elegant Junction that boasted 44 train routes every day. Railroad contractors had completed the Hannibal to St. Joseph Railway ahead of schedule in 1859 and each man earned a bonus; ten gallons of whiskey. My daddy, Joshua, would walk along the train tracks and pick up the pieces of coal that had fallen off the top of the over-loaded coal cars. He would fill up a big burlap bag with coal, bring it home, and use this coal to heat our home during the extreme cold of Missouri winters.

One day, a railroad man who worked for a train line spotted my dad picking up the coal.

"Hey, what are you doing, boy?" the man shouted, while briskly walking closer. He obviously knew what Joshua was doing, and Daddy instantly sensed the provocative behavior that occupied certain white men in those days who enjoyed exercising hate-filled dominance with positions of undue authority. These are the insecure, juvenile bullies who live by base agendas that serve no purpose other than to satisfy an inner thirst for violence. These are men who exercised violent acts on black men without even knowing why...

"You're on private property, boy!" He was now about fifty yards away but approaching fast. "Where I'm from, that's called stealin', boy."

Joshua instinctively knew to move quickly to throw off the charge from this type of man whose character doesn't like to reason. As the man walked closer, putting his hand on the pistol that railroad men were allowed to carry, Joshua knew that this wasn't about the value of coal or protecting trains.

With one swift move, Joshua dumped the bag, wheeled towards town, and shouted over his shoulder, "I'll just have to go get the sheriff..."

Stumped by Joshua's reaction, the railroad man stopped for a moment in confusion. This wasn't the ordinary cooperative response he had expected from a black man who was being harassed.

"Yeah, the sheriff told me to come up here and clean up the terrible mess that you railroad guys are always making with your coal falling off the trains." Daddy walked quickly, almost trotting, as he glanced backward. "I'll just have the sheriff come up here and talk to you 'bout stopping me from doing my duties."

48

It worked. The railroad man stood frozen, unsure of what to do, as Joshua disappeared over a hill.

Daddy stopped picking up coal for a little while after that. But, after some time had passed, I guess Joshua got tired of seeing the coal sit there slowly disintegrating into the elements of the weather, so he began to pick it up again, warily keeping a watchful eye out for racist railroad workers.

Daddy hated to see things of value go to waste, especially when his family could hardly eat at times. He frequently tried to reap the benefits of what white folks would throw into the garbage. But, if Daddy got caught taking anything home, many whites got irritated that it didn't get thrown away for some reason. Hmm, crazy to me... But it seemed that those particular kind of white folks would rather the dogs or the landfill have it before a black man.

On another occasion, my daddy had finished working for twelve hours to clean up a white woman's entire property. He sat down in the shade to rest. Within two minutes, the woman came running out of the house as if it were on fire.

"What are you doing?" she asked with her hands on her hips.

"I'm just takin' me a quick break, ma'am," Joshua calmly told her.

She left for a quick second, emerged with a pair of pruners in her hand, and handed them to daddy. "Well, prune on these bushes back here while you're resting," she said wryly.

And so it was in the extremely difficult life in the community for my daddy. But he never seemed to let it bother him. He kept his eye on the ball, and the ball was keeping us with food, clothes, and shelter. He was watchful against any source that might threaten that. These sources included blacks as well as whites, and professionals as well as transients. Daddy was even mistrustful of the black deacon from the local white church.

Joshua knew that the white church used the black deacon to attract blacks to the congregation. The black population was sparse and poor in our small-town community, but they were known as the top givers to a God they feared. Though Daddy didn't attend church much, the deacon dropped by one day in his nice suit, took a look around, and seemed to be fishing for a contribution. My daddy, who was changing the oil on his "dump truck", stood up to greet the conniving minister.

The deacon stood far enough away so as to not have to shake hands. He wanted his suit to stay clean. "Are you raising any of these chickens for the Lord?" the deacon asked with a sly grin.

Daddy, instantly sensing the purpose for his visit, answered quickly, "A few for the Lord, a few for Joshua, but none for the deacon!"

And that was the end of that. The deacon sadly walked away and never asked Daddy for a handout again.

As all of us children came into the world, my daddy kept working at the same steady, arduous pace. He disappeared for a spell, when I was six-years-old, when Daddy had to go overseas for the war. But before the war or after, I don't remember Joshua sitting around much. I also don't remember him being too emotional about anything. We may have had to eat bacon grease with beans for dinner, but Mamma always cooked it and Joshua always brought it home.

Daddy had a down-to-earth, business-like approach to life, and I suppose he had to, with the way things were...

In 1929, Mary Ellen had been the first baby to come into the Jackson home. Mom and Dad had enjoyed the festive hoopla that a first baby brings into a childless home, but that would only last five days as Mary Ellen died due to a breathing ailment of some kind. Only God knows the "when and why" of a person's time and departure into eternity. The ones who are left to mourn must endure the shock of loss and the endless questions that follow. Some apply the questions to the dead, some to themselves, and most apply them to both. In black homes, the shock and questions don't seem to last as long...

Death seems to always be a steadfast companion, his dark presence being much more familiar because of the more frequent visits.

In 1930, George had been born. Three years later, I came next. And, shortly after my birth, the twins, Orville and Norville, were attempting to make their appearance into this world. But during the birth, my daddy heard their necks pop and they were pronounced dead.

In those days, a mid-wife, and possibly a doctor, would come into the home for the baby deliveries. On this day, there was only a mid-wife, a local white lady who specialized in the delivery of calves for farmers. Yep... you heard me right! A white lady who specialized in the delivery of baby calves. She simply shook her head after the failed births, offered her condolences as she washed her hands in the sink, took her things, and then left.

A difficult and semi-necessary cost for many black families was life insurance for their dead. A modest, inexpensive box would do for the burial of older loved ones who had lived a full life. For the tiny stillborn, even this decision was optional, and the laws of the land reflected such. So Joshua took their limp, little bodies and gently laid them into a hole that he had dug in the backyard.

He had tried to soothe my mom as she lay in bed staring at the ceiling. With a quivering lower lip, and sweat dotting her brow, she refused to blink, even as a tear emerged. After a few hours, her breathing returned to a calm and normal pace. But it would take time for her spirit to do the same. "I'm okay," she finally whispered without looking at Daddy. "Go bury the boys."

Daddy knew she wasn't well. He knew she was not okay.

No one knew what my daddy was thinking as he picked up his shovel while standing over the two newest members of our family. He began to toss dirt on their lifeless bodies. Afterwards, he stood fixated, looking down at them for a long time... He remained motionless, as stiff as a statue. He didn't cry. He had no expression. Lost in loneliness, he reflected his grief by looking at the nearby weeping willow. Joshua had sat under this tree many times while trying to cope with the anguish that often accompanied black men removed from their homeland. It was close to a distant cornfield where a breeze gently made its way over the passage... blowing while lightly swaying the tree's branches.

He may have imagined what the two twins would become... He may have imagined them running into heaven... He may have imagined the eternal rest that they were now experiencing, the same rest that he often longed for. Maybe Daddy had even been thinking of what he could say to my mother... what words would possibly make her feel better? Why did God seem so distant?

Death seemed to blend in with the common day... the birds, the trees, the wind... all paying no attention... carrying out their natural duties... oblivious to the burdens of man.

Whatever Joshua was thinking, he took his time. Even after the sun slowly sank behind the field, Daddy stood there, frozen, a strong man with a humbled heart and slumping shoulders... unsure or unwilling to do what would come next... a shovel in his right hand.

If I didn't know my daddy, I would say he looked slightly defeated. But that was not his nature, nor an option. The sky was now red, as Joshua looked towards the heavens for answers. Where were the beautiful portraits in the sky? Where was God's awesome

Hand at this time? With bloodshot eyes and a secret urgency, he scanned carefully from horizon to horizon. But the sky was clear and silent. Light from the distant stars above the sky began to shine into focus. A full moon began to peak over the trees. The crickets began to make their usual racket... Joshua took one last look into the hole, but it was now too dark to see what remained of the two little bodies.

Joshua briefly closed his eyes and took a deep breath before scooping the last pile of dirt... He turned and splashed it on top of their two little faces. The dirt hit suddenly, blending perfectly with their color of lifelessness. The bodies of Orville and Norville disappeared from the light forever.

Daddy's wordless "good-bye" was interrupted by the cruel movement of time.

7

"Black Home in a White Town"

"Ahhhhhhhhhhhhhhhh" Mamma screamed. She paused for a second, panting heavily, sweat dripping down her face. "Is he almost out?" No answer. "Joshua! Clarissa!"

Joshua peeked into the room. "How should I know?" he asked. "The midwife is right there." It seemed that daddy learned to keep out of the room during births, but he listened attentively and kept a watchful eye outside the doorway. It also seemed that he considered himself as bad luck or some sort of curse, especially after the death of the twins.

It didn't take long for me to learn the name of the midwife... Clarissa. First, she became a rather consistent presence in our home. And, besides, I thought she was better than her real livelihood as a baby calf specialist. It seemed Mamma was pregnant or giving birth for twenty straight years!

"Almost..." Clarissa said softly. "One more push, Sarina..." Even Clarissa seemed a bit nervous, considering the bad fortune of dying babies for Mamma and Daddy; but this birth was different. Clarissa seemed excessively distracted also. I saw lots of blood...

The baby came out. It was a boy, and Sarina had decided to name him Ephraim.

Not counting my twin who died at birth, the buried twins were the fourth and fifth babies of Joshua and Sarina. Ephraim was number six. He was born premature and only weighed three pounds at birth. Clarissa wrapped the baby with some torn rags that we kept around the house for diapers, and then handed him to Joshua.

'Kind of tiny, ain't he?' was Daddy's first thought as he looked down at the newborn baby. Fitting snug into Daddy's hands, baby Ephraim sneezed.

Clarissa's attention wasn't on the baby. She couldn't stop the bleeding, and Mamma just lay there sleeping. I had never seen Clarissa so nervous. Filled with anxiety, she ran around the room grabbing more rags. "Go get the doctor, Betty!" Clarissa finally screamed.

I darted out of the room and ran to Dr. Wagner's office that was about a half-mile away. I burst into the door, where a sixty-something, gray-haired, white doctor was sticking an ice cream stick into a woman's mouth as though he was checking her tonsils. Flirting with her, he glanced over her shoulder through his reading glasses. Dr. Wagner seemed alarmed then annoyed after he saw it was me. Although sensing that this was a bad time for an interruption, I didn't care because I knew Mamma needed my help.. and fast.

Out of breath and out of time, I suddenly blurt out, "Doctor, my mamma's bleeding real bad!" I managed a couple of quick breaths before adding, "She just had a baby and the midwife sent me up here to fetch you."

"Can't you see I'm busy with this woman's sore throat?" Dr. Wagner said calmly, smiling at the woman. I noticed right away that she was the lady from the other side of town. My mamma knew her, and I had seen her come to many of our family picnics.

The doctor slowly took off his glasses and placed them into his shirt pocket. He whispered a few more things to her and added a wink. The woman smiled back, glanced over at me, stood up, and then walked out the door.

Dr. Wagner frowned at me and continued to take his time. "Please sit down outside and I will be with you when I've finished gathering my things".

Dr. Wagner's reaction to my request was as if I had asked for something that was unwarranted.

This was the first time I can actually remember being angry, really angry, at the arrogant reaction of a white person. Even at my young age, I understood how inappropriate the doctor's uncaring demeanor was in an emergency.

"No, Doctor Wagner," I said firmly and loudly. "My mamma needs you now... right now!"

He stared at me and frowned at my sense of urgency.

"You're being rather rude, Betty," the doctor said. He gathered his composure and managed to take me more seriously.

"What if yo' mamma was bleedin', sir?"

As a girl, growing up in a white society... I could never understand why a black person's behavior was questioned whenever they demanded to be treated fairly... or like an actual person. Instead of addressing the reason for my panic, the doctor redirected his attention away from me. It didn't matter the cause. He made me feel like my feelings had no relevance.

I walked outside confused and angry, while thinking, *Will mom be okay?*

I thought by now, Clarissa and Daddy were probably wondering what was taking so long. "Why didn't she send Daddy, and let me hold the baby," I muttered to myself? Instantly, I knew. The doctor would probably make Daddy mad with his rude actions, and Daddy's reaction to that would probably land him in jail. I paced the front porch of his small office, while thinking of my options. I could get the sheriff, but his reaction would probably be even worse or slower. Besides, mamma needed a doctor, and the sheriff getting the doctor would just be another hurdle. I waited and paced, my stomach growing tighter and tighter with knots.

Finally, fifteen minutes later, the doctor came out with his eyes gazing across the street at the woman who had just moments ago left his office. She was slowly walking her way back to the other "side of town". Clicking her high heels on the pavement as if she wanted to attract more attention to herself. Men drove by as they turned their heads.

Dr. Wagner calmly took his keys and locked the office door.

"Come on," I finally spewed impatiently. I felt like a volcano that needed to erupt and, by now, my stomach was hurting terribly.

"I'm giving up my lunch time for this," the doctor grunted, while searching for his car keys.

If I knew how and didn't think it would hurt Mamma more, I would have punched that doctor right in his eye. I stood there waiting while I imagined ways of losing my temper with that doctor, but I understood I was experiencing a crash course in understanding the black man's hostility. He had to protect and at the same time work for his family against all the odds of a white society favored. And he had to keep his justified anger under control or explode. Far too many times black men explode, and our prisons' populations reflect the unfair choices of his plight.

I walked swiftly ahead. About halfway home, I mumbled to myself what was on my mind to that doctor. "If my Mamma was white, you would be hurrying like you was goin' to put out a fire at your house, Mr. Wagner!"

"How dare you!" I imagined he'd say. "Betty, I'm not moving until you apologize for this ridiculous attack on me!"

Oh, how a wrongdoer can flip the tables while hiding the double standards of the heart, I thought. *Maybe they actually believe their righteous façade.* I thought again, '*Why, when a white person is assertive, they are an advocate for the hurting? But, when a black person is assertive, they are an attacker and unruly.*

Mamma nearly died that day.

During the week, Daddy found other doctors to come by, while trying to care for the new baby at the same time. Each doctor came out of the house with the same shake of the head, informing Joshua that Mamma wasn't going to make it and that his secretary would send him a bill for services by mail next week. Then a preacher from Saint Joseph showed up. He anointed Mamma's head with oil and calmly pronounced her as healed in the Name of Jesus.

Mamma made it through. But immediately after that brush with death, a huge, cancerous knot formed and was eating at my mamma's neck. When the tumor was removed at Missouri Methodist Hospital, I could see the inside of my mother's throat. Many doctors and preachers continued to come by the house. This time, I even overheard a preacher say as he was leaving, "I wouldn't give a nickel for her life…" But, again, Mamma made it through.

As soon as she was strong enough, Mamma went back to her resourceful self. She mixed a certain kind of concoction to feed to baby Ephraim so that he could grow. Ephraim grew bigger and stronger. Before long, he had grown to be the size and weight of a healthy, normal child.

As I reminisce on my childhood, many things that may be considered strange today were just part of life back then. We ate freshly-killed possums, groundhogs, and raccoons that Daddy shot. We all sat on a homemade sled that a horse pulled to escort us in the winters.

There was always mud on your feet. The roads were dirt, and the floors of our home were dirt, too. We made a Christmas tree from tree branches that we assembled together. We had a wood stove that heated the home although the dirt floors stayed cold. We always made do with whatever the Lord gave us, no matter how small, and we were thankful for it. We knew only what we knew. And, because we had no television, and didn't go over the white kids' homes, we didn't know if we had it tough, even if we did. Rags for diapers, beds made out of straw with coats thrown on top, wood and coal fires, lamp and lanterns, crowded beds with elbows in your ribs and bare feet next to your face; all of these were just a wonderful part of life for us. If we were poor, we didn't know it. We only knew when our bellies got empty, but there was always something to be thrown together to temporarily fill them... again.. and then again...

We were never far from fun or an adventure. We competed against each other as we fished for food. We rode bareback on our horses, racing them into the open field with the wind in our hair. And we spent many a summer day at the swimming hole or reservoir, because the swimming pool in Cameron was "for white folks only". We also played a lot of horseshoes, an inexpensive game that never seemed to get old to us.

Our home was a two-story house with a cellar that Daddy had bought after he received his bonus check from World War I, which was about $300. It was right in the middle of all the activities. Downtown Cameron was close. The city park was close. The pool was close. And the spot where all the festivals, carnivals, and fourth of July fireworks was literally right outside our door! I loved that all the people would cut through our yard to get to the ballgames or sit on our front lawn to watch the fireworks. On one side of us was the old College Farm, though it was about a block away. On the other side of us was the Williams' farm, and it was about two blocks away. So our single acre and home sat fairly isolated with lots of open fields around it. The fields were owned by others, but there weren't a lot of other homes in our immediate area.

After Ephraim was born and Mamma was healed of her throat dilemma, the babies just kept right on comin'. Dan was next. Daddy nicknamed him "Diffy" because Dan was so different.

But he was sharp. From his birth, he was a quick thinker.

Then came child number seven, Esther. She was born with the gift in a powerful way. Esther had so much life, and yet she possessed the same serious trait to her that a lot of us had. One day, little Esther was walking around, stumbling in a fashion that toddlers do, when one of the roosters jumped on top of her. That rooster flapped its wings and made a racket, as it had little Esther down on the ground crying. Daddy Joshua walked up, grabbed the rooster, and quickly wrung its neck. As he tossed the dead rooster to the side and helped Esther up, he uttered, "We ain't even gonna' eat it," before walking off.

About a year later, came Evelyn. As soon as she could, she talked a lot. Everyone called her little "chatterbox". The number ten child was Lawrence. Lawrence was the best little kid. He was like an angel. After Lawrence, came Joshua Euell, named after our daddy's uncle. Of course, he was also Joshua, Jr., but everyone called him Butchy.

Daddy didn't talk much about his uncle Joshua, although he had been named after him. It was known throughout the family that Uncle Josh had died in jail in Saint Joseph, Missouri. And, although the death certificate mocked that "timbers fell on his head" as the cause of death, the rumor had circulated in Northwest Missouri that Uncle Josh had killed himself in the jail. Of course, no one believed the authorities and had given up on reaching the truth. Uncle Josh was dead, and the uncertainty, injustice, and frustration of accessing truth all amounted to an accepted code of silence from both sides.

My daddy and his daddy were not stupid. They knew what happened. But, even if they could prove it, in those days, there wasn't much of anything that anyone could do about it. Secret, or not so secret, murders of local black men were a common part of every police department's storied history. A family either accepted the injustice and went on, or they constantly thought and talked about it until the bitterness began to eat at them, day after day. Our family chose to let it go… The alternative usually resulted in future incidents of abuse …

Two years after Butchy was born, came the twelfth and last baby, Everett Francis. He, too, was very smart. From an extraordinarily young age, he always read books. An intellectual seriousness seemed to invade the soul of such a young child. But that's who he was. He was intent on matters that were usually contemplated by those well beyond his years. He would just sit there and observe. No matter how silly the antics, even if it was a sing-song poem made up by "chatterbox" Evelyn June, he would sit there, take it all in, and frown. There always seemed to be someone else much older inside him.

As our family grew, we were often joined by Mamma's siblings and their kids, as well as my daddy's side of the family and local friends. That's another thing that I thank God for; each other. We were never bored. We could sit on the porch, in the grass, or under a tree anytime and have someone to laugh with, tell enticing stories to, or argue with. The adults would "play the dozens" on week-end nights when most didn't have to work the next day. Many of us kids would hide, listen, and laugh at the entertainment brought into our home, especially by the hilarious young men teasing each other, while the older men played cards around the table as they drank carelessly into the night.

"Playing the dozens" was what we called it when we would all sit around, the more the merrier, and make fun of each other in a friendly, teasing way. Or we would make fun of a family member in somebody's bloodline. The game would sometimes start with the old saying, "I don't play the dozens 'cause the dozens is bad, but I could tell you how many children your great-grandmother had!" Then the "insults" would begin. Most times, "the dozens" just started up innocently and naturally picked up full steam later.

"Man, you so bad of a shot, all the coons feel safe to come and eat right at yo' dinner table. You still can't hit 'em. That's why all them holes in yo' walls..." Haaa, the folks in the room might rate your insult by the length of their "haaaaa" or there might be a burst of laughter, especially if there were real holes in one of our relative's wall put there by somebody's crazy uncle trying to shoot a rat.

Those in the "gallery" not participating might also add little comments like, "That's true... He do got a lotta' holes in his walls... Sho' nuff..."

Then it would be the time for the challenger to slap back his insult.

"Yeah, well, yo' right, yo' right", he would begin as the laughter died down and the anticipation re-built. Then he would come with his shot like a counter-punching boxer. "You know, they say you're the greatest hunter in the woods... You can't shoot a gun straight, but all the animals fall over dead as you walk past 'em... 'cause of yo' nasty stinking feet!" he'd yell. "And go put some deodorant on!!!!"

"Haaaaaaa..."

The two of them would go back and forth for a time, while others waited to take a shot. This night, a "defender" chimed in, because the floor was always open.

"Yeah, well, at least my mamma didn't scare the kids right out of the church! Yeah, you all didn't hear? His mamma was praisin' the Lord, and her fake wig fell off the back of her head and hooked onto the back of her belt. When her butt moved, everyone thought Uncle Jed's horse had wandered into the church! When she flipped, everyone ran out of the church saying yo' mamma gots a demon!!! Yo' mamma's butt's as big as the deep, blue ocean! No wonder Uncle Jed's crazy!!!"

The Dozens didn't have to always make perfect sense. The length of laughter usually depended on the comedic timing or how much booze was in the listeners...

"Haaaaaaaaaa...."

"Well, least my mamma goes to church. Since yo' mamma started her own cathouse... Well, let's just say at least we know where to find all the preachers in Clinton County now..."

"Oh... Ouch... Look out now... Haaaaaaaaaa..."

This night, my six-year-old cousin walked in and shouted in his high voice, "Yeah, well, least my mamma's boobies ain't all over the place!"

If something wasn't funny, there was silence. "Ohhh, man, shut up..."

But the game would soon pick right back up.

"Get yo' dwarf, crumb-eatin', funny-wanna-bein' butt back to yo' own kind," one of the players growled, aiming at a young cousin that just arrived with a white women. "Ain't it past yo' bedtime, pint-size? This here's for grown-folk... Don't you have a cuppa' milk at the kiddie table? It's midnight!! Where's yo' mamma anyway?"

"Playing the dozens" might go on for hours into the night. Usually the family members took it all in fun, because they knew each other so well. Once in a while, a non-family member or new in-law might try to join in. Or someone might have had a little too much to drink. Or, God forbid, someone might try to sneak in some offensive drama that was really happening. If someone ended up getting mad, we would call that "jumpin' salty".

So, in the morning, there might be a report like, "Yeah, the Dozens was playin' strong until Johnny jumped salty!" And that report would mean that the jokes were especially entertaining until Johnny ended up getting mad.

Many famous black comics, such as Dick Gregory and Eddie Murphy, more than likely came out of homes and backgrounds where they witnessed various versions of "the Dozens" night after night from their never-famous, unknown-to-the-world uncles, cousins, and other family members. But the purpose, back then, wasn't to make money or even to be funny. It was a form of therapy. All the stresses of the day would disappear with the easy laughter that the Dozens brought to the oppressed. Mostly, there were few rules and an underlying form of acceptance, fun, and love, so the playing could really get going.

Many players might walk on the edge of social injustice, using their words like recipes with a gallon of exaggeration mixed with "a cup of truth" and sprinkled with just a teaspoon of anger. This night, Daddy's friend, Nate leaned in close and lowered his voice. This meant that his "play" was against a white man or he didn't want his wife, who was in the next room with the other women, hearing him. "Yeah, you know the preacher at the First Baptist? The wrinkled one that look like a shriveled raisin? Yeah, he didn't know I was there, and I saw him countin' the money while takin' out his own tithes." Then Nate stood up and mocked the preacher. He looked around like a criminal, seeing if anyone was around before mimicking an invisible stack of money. "One fo' dem, nine fo' me, none fo' dem, nine fo' me..."

Nate's wife peeked in, and he hurriedly sat down until she disappeared into the kitchen.

"Haaaaaaaaaaaaaaaaaaaaa… sho' nuff… Yep, that's how he be countin'… Look out now… Haaaaaaaa…"

"Haaaa…. You know that's how they do… Haaaaaaa!"

But usually the game was light-hearted and entertaining. On a good night, everyone would join in, and the cares of life and misfortune would be long forgotten. On a good night, the exaggerations would get wilder and wilder. Two animated family members might go back and forth for a long time, even jumping up and imitating the movements of their targets. The role-playing would be epic comedy. You could even hear loud talking and laughter as the company listened from the other room.

If we weren't playing the Dozens, Daddy could always tell us a story that would have us all laughing hysterically. Some were told over and over. There was the one about Aunt Dino. "Ol, Aunt Dino," Daddy would start. He would stand up, put on one of my mamma's church hats, and switch his hips around the room with exaggeration. He would stick his hand in the air as if he were praising God. Then he would start his shrill voice to mimic hers. "I'm a Lawd-lovin', foot-washin', Baptist Princess bound for glory! Thank 'ya, Lawd!"

Everyone would start clapping and start getting into it…

"Well, let's have a dance contest, Aunt Dino…" Daddy shouted in his regular voice, switching roles and taking the hat off. "Third-place prize is a Dominicker hen…"

Putting the hat back on, he would mimic Aunt Dino as an offended female with his hands on his hips. "'Ain't gonna' be no dancing 'round here," said Aunt Dino.

'Why not, Aunt Dino?'

'Cause I'm a Lawd-lovin', foot-washin', Baptist Princess bound for glory, that's why not! Thank ya, Lawd!'

'Well, Aunt Dino, second-place prize is a big 'ol bottle of Holland's gin!'

'I said, ain't gonna' be no dancin' or drinkin' 'round here!'

'Well, why not, Aunt Dino?'

'Cause I'm a Lawd-lovin', foot-washin', Baptist Princess bound for glory, that's why not, you heathen! Thank ya, Jeeeeezus!'

'Okay, well, Aunt Dino, first-place prize… is a big, fat, juicy possum smothered in gravy and sweet potatoes!'

'What're we waitin' for?' yelled Aunt Dino with waving arms and big eyes. 'Get the music ready!'"

We would all laugh no matter how old the story got, no matter how many times told...

Another story Daddy told was about this ugly woman who wanted to get married. "A man told her, 'Go on top of the roof and I'll marry you tonight'. So she went on top of the roof and waited." "Midnight!" Daddy bellowed in anger like a distraught woman. "Cold, so cold… Gonna' be mad in the morning. One o'clock in the morning! Cold, so cold… Gonna' be mad in the morning…" Daddy would go on and on, each hour, until he reached seven o'clock, and then he shook like someone freezing. "Seven o'clock in the morning!" he shrieked, shaking and nodding groggily. "Then she froze and fell off the roof!"

For some reason, though there was nothing unusually funny about an ugly, cold, tired woman falling off of a roof, we laughed every time, as Daddy imitated the woman reeling downward.

Then there would be the stories about "the gift". When we shared stories about the gift, we usually only did it around family. No one else would understand, or they would think we were perhaps lying. The gift referred to our supernatural sightings and voices in the spiritual realm. We listened to each other's dreams, visions, and other happenings with serious awe and reverence. We dared not diverge these descriptions with loud or fast talking. Our voices were as hushed and precise as a desperate prayer, and our audience was our church.

To us, this is how God spoke to our family. This was the Master Himself sharing with us a piece of Him. To the outside world, we may have been "darkies", them making us a lower form of humanity, our skin color reflecting some sort of defect or a tragic misfortune of nature. But the Creator gave us a gift to see a spiritual world that was hidden from most everyone else.

Amazing. He didn't care what color we were; He saw our beauty and blessed our hearts. This was our time to hear from the living God. For Him to share this "gift" with us? Well, it was finally time for us to feel favored, to feel supreme in a way. We listened to insight to mysteries of Life and Death. And we spent many evenings trusting each other with that glorious homage that He entrusted us with.

Daddy Joshua was as witty as he was resourceful. But, most of all, he had "life smarts", the commonsense intellect to be able to, not just survive, but thrive by fully maximizing whatever resources the Lord brought within our grasp. I followed him and learned.

One day, as Daddy was changing a belt on his trash hauler, he turned to me and said, "Now, Betty, you learn from history…" He stopped and looked off someplace, before shaking a wrench towards me to emphasize the importance of his statement. "… so as to not make the same mistakes again and again. Learn!"

"I know that Abraham Lincoln set us free, Daddy…" I said to show off.

"No, that's what I'm talking about. 'Ol Lincoln didn't set us free, God did. It was time. He might've used Lincoln and others, but it was time, just like when God used Moses to bring His Children out of Egypt."

Daddy didn't have a lot of schooling, but he learned things from having listened to a black man that the locals called Professor Ridge.

Among the basics of history, he would teach my dad that most of the main characters in the bible looked like us , including Jesus. Professor Ridge had a PhD in history and taught at many colleges in the South. But his teaching was just too radical and accurate for many to accept. Never would he get a job teaching at a white college. But, strangely, he was eventually terminated from many of the black colleges. Professor Ridge retired and moved up into our quiet Missouri area. Though he taught about American and other history for over forty years, he lived in a very small shack somewhere down by the railroad tracks near the woods. But whoever came his way, he taught them, and he seemed to enjoy teaching curious men like my daddy for hours on end, or just as long as they could stand it.

"Well, how you know that Lincoln didn't do it by himself?" I asked. "He was the president, right?"

"Too many evil men, Betty," Daddy said slowly, tightening the hauler belt. "He didn't have the support. Plus, there's a side to Lincoln that most don't know. Did you know that he wanted to move all the colored folks down to a poor part of the world called Panama? He invited five black leaders to the White House and tried talking them into telling their people to leave this country. He told them black leaders, 'If it weren't for y'all, we wouldn't of had a war'".

"We were forced here from Africa, weren't we?" I asked. "How was the war our fault?"

"Now, see that?" Daddy said, smiling. "Even a child knows how stupid that sounds. Ain't that somethin', Betty? In 1860, 80 percent of this here gross national product was tied to slavery. And, after we got free, they wanted to toss us out to South America like garbage. And, not only did they want to tell us, 'Hey, we done with y'all, and thanks a lot for many years of free labor to make us internationally wealthy', but then they wanted to add, 'Oh, and by the way, that big 'ol war that destroyed half our country? Yeah, that was y'all's fault.' Yeah, Lincoln didn't exactly want us to rise up and be equal on all counts. Hell, he didn't even want us to stay. It was Frederick Douglass, a black man, whispering in ol' Lincoln's ear, that talked him into lettin' us stay and fight for the Union. Without Douglass in the background, Lincoln wouldn't have been Lincoln. And even the war might've turned out differently... Most of the inventions were made by black slaves, while the white masters got the credit..."

"Well, how come we ain't learnin' that at our school?"

"Cause you learning from them white books, Betty."

Though our family loved to read, write, and learn, and though we played with the white kids all summer long, the schools in Missouri were segregated. It was required that it took a minimum of five kids to start a school in those days. The white school in Cameron was a beautifully designed, huge brick building. The black school was named Douglas School. But it was really only a small rooming house by the railroad tracks that had been for the black porters and other black servants to stay who worked on the passenger railway cars. It leaked horribly in the rain, and, when a significant storm came through, we were sent home.

When the books, desks, tables, and other school necessities were too raggedy for the white schools, we got them. The white schools would even send their leftover food to us for lunch, only after they had finished. That's probably why we were always learning from the "white people's books".

I had started in the black school when I was five-years-old. We barely had the five-person minimum. There were my cousins, James, Robert Tapps, and Frank Suggs... my brother, George, and then me. We were all five-years-old, except for George and my cousin, Robert, who were both seven. The few other black kids in town were either working already in the fields with their families to help provide food on the table, or their parents didn't emphasize education as a vital priority.

Our teacher was a nice, black woman by the name of Miss Ridge. I remember only bits and pieces of my few years in school. I remember learning the "Pledge of Allegiance" and the "23rd Psalm" from the bible. I remember during lunch hour when a white man arrived bringing the leftovers from the white school. I remember learning math and the extraordinarily tedious hours that our part-time math teacher Miss Fine spent with us making sure we could do basic addition and subtraction. Before long, however, we would go back to engage yet again into the learning and reading about what was in the "white history books" with the inaccuracies that Daddy pointed out.

"The bible, Betty," Daddy would say at times. "The very words of God. The bible is the only book on this here planet that you can trust, Betty. It's the only pure one, the only accurate one all the way through. Every other book is tainted for the intended purpose of the writer or whoever hired the writer. Every other book's got a bias, whether intended or not, 'cause we people are flawed in the first place. The bible is the only book that is completely objective and truthful. You want to know something accurately? Go to the bible. You want to know how to survive? How to be happy? How to love? How to get along? How... to... live... forever? Go to the bible, Betty."

One day I decided to be ornery. "But, Daddy, didn't men write the bible?"

"The Holy Spirit wrote the bible," Daddy answered with a frown, as if he was disappointed in himself for not teaching me that yet.

"Why the books in the bible got authors then, like Matthew?"

Daddy looked at me carefully. "Let's say you are Matthew," he began, pointing his big index finger at me. "And I tell you every word to write down... And then you do it... Now who wrote the book?"

"Matthew," I said, again just to challenge.

"But whose words are they, Betty?" He saw my grin, and knew that I was joking, and quickly finished his lesson. "Matthew and the rest were just secretaries taking notation. That's why every author, no matter what time period, agreed perfectly with each other. It wasn't their words. They was all told what to write... Wrote what they saw."

I also remember something that scared me at the school. When a train went by, a thick, black smoke would fill the area around our school while we were inside the classroom. I didn't tell anyone and didn't want anyone to know it, but, for whatever reason, that black smoke always frightened me immensely! I would stand paralyzed, frozen with fear, blind to all my surroundings, until that black smoke lifted away, which sometimes seemed to take forever.

The black smoke from the loud trains taught me something though... You can stand or walk in complete darkness, but just keep going until it eventually clears away. I learned that the smoke itself could never hurt me; it could only get me to hurt myself inside my head. Sooner or later, the darkness always cleared. I learned to hang on, trust, and keep going until it did...

One evening, I told Daddy about my victory over the black smoke... how I learned to wait until it cleared away along with my fears.

"That's good, Betty," he said, while throwing down chicken feed. "That's a real good lesson you taught yo'self. Just feel sorry for all them folks in hell."

I wondered why Daddy would say that. I knew all the characteristics of hell. A couple of years prior, Daddy had put a thick blindfold on me and slowly walked me closer and closer to the bonfire he had going until I couldn't take feeling the darkness or heat anymore. He did this after I had asked what hell felt like. My heart pounded with terror. He took the blindfold off, and moved me away from the fire, before adding, "And it's a whole lot worse than that, Betty..."

"Why you feel sorry for the folks in hell when I talk about the black train smoke?" I now asked.

"'Cause for them, Betty, the darkness and the fear never, ever lifts. They just got to stay in it... Always treat people kind, Betty. Don't ever mistreat people because of their color..."

When I look back, we were raised to be pretty tough physically. I remember when my brother, Ephraim, at about nine-years-old, had a pitchfork go completely through his foot. After that, he got the tetanus disease. He began to feel a tightening in his jaw and great pain in his neck. I felt sorry for him, as he would moan and groan in the midst of mini convulsions, his eyes popping wide, his jaw tense, and noises coming from his mouth along with some kind of strange spit. I looked to mom and dad, who never seemed to panic. They seemed to know what was happening. The doctor came in and poured medicine on the wound, but it went right through his foot and onto the dirt floor. When the convulsions ended, Ephraim would politely look the doctor in the eye. He didn't even cry. I remember being so scared for my brother as another "episode" began to come.

"Why don't you do somethin'?" I screamed at the doctor, as Ephraim began twisting violently while making strange noises.

Daddy took my arm and escorted me outside. He bent down and looked me in the eyes.

"Look here, Betty," he said, as I fought back the tears. "Fear and anger don't never make nothin' better. They make panic, and that only makes you do foolish things."

Eventually the infection went away, the convulsions stopped, and Ephraim was outside again running carelessly throughout the countryside. I remember his progress was the best immediately after the visits from the black church folks.

It was a regular routine that I recalled more than a few times... A doctor would walk out of our house with his head shaking in confusion, and then a line of church believers would start coming from the other direction into our house. With their heads held high, their angelic faces chiseled with hopeful assurance.

For a time, my childhood in Cameron was a good one. Though Daddy felt the daily sting of racial hatred, he desperately tried to made sure that it never fell on his children. Summers were filled with fun and games with the white kids. Evenings were the time when family assembled on the front porch, as the orange sun lowered majestically onto center stage, flaunting unknown colors and never-seen patterns in the sky, dwarfing the vast farmland below in a grand display that stretched to the horizon. Sometimes the lights over the ball field would glow onto the buzzing fans as the Junction Greasers, the local baseball team, took the field against other towns' teams from all over Missouri and Kansas. I can remember the excitement I felt as the blowing trees waved, ushering in ominous clouds. I remember the rain and sizzling flashes of light from the West. At times, when God chose, a twisting tornado would lightly appear, dancing on the distant hills, exiting the stage to the North.

Most of all, I remember family. We weren't real strong-going church people, but God always seemed close. Daddy had always taught us to never lie. We get a good whuppin' for sure if we were caught misrepresenting the truth in any way. I remember how death just seemed a part of life to us. I also recall how Mom would warn us about witchcraft. "Watch what you eat," she would say, Daddy's stern face nodding behind her in agreement. In those days, casting spells was a common way of destroying enemies. "Watch who you trust. Don't take a part in witchcraft, or it will come back to get you later. And don't hate! Hatred is like witchcraft. Hatred is like casting spells…"

Fridays were the days that I stayed after school with Miss Ridge to help clean. I couldn't wait to tell her what I had learned "outside of the books" from Daddy.

"Miss Ridge, did you know that Mr. Lincoln wanted to send black folks to South America?" I asked innocently, as I kept my eyes on the blackboard I was washing.

"President Lincoln, you mean?" she asked. "Who told you that lie?"

"My daddy told me that there's a whole lot we don't know because we're always learning from them white books about history…"

"And where did your daddy learn from?" she asked with a smile.

"He says he learned from a man named Professor Ridge…"

Suddenly, I heard the shattering of a thick, glass vase that Miss Ridge had been cleaning. It broke loudly onto the stained floor. She looked at me with a shocked look of concern that I had never seen on Miss Ridge's face before.

"You don't listen to anyone who learned from Professor Ridge," she said, her hands slightly shaking as she calmed herself and began picking up the glass pieces. "He ain't nothin' but an old vagrant… an old, broken-down, homeless vagrant that lives down by the tracks."

"My daddy says he lives in a shack…"

"He's homeless!" Miss Ridge spewed out obstinately. She looked upset. Then, after a small delay, she bent down again to finish gathering the broken glass. "Just don't listen to him… or anyone that repeats what he says. He's… crazy. An old, crazy, homeless man…"

74

I later found out that Professor Ridge was Miss Ridge's daddy. It turned out that they weren't real close, because, down South, Professor Ridge had gotten arrested due to many "made-up" accusations from KKK members who didn't like his teaching. There's one lesson I learned about slavery. When it was abolished, white Southerners still needed people to work the land. So they would arrest black men for tiny or made-up infractions, such as vagrancy, and make them work on the chain gangs. This was legalized, manipulated slavery but manpower nonetheless... It turns out that Miss Ridge and her mamma had left the South for Missouri while Professor Ridge was incarcerated. But, after being freed, he found out where his daughter had moved, and he moved up to the same town to be close to her. Still, it would be a while before I would learn what upset their relationship.

I always thanked God for these early years in Cameron. But I can't describe the feeling that I had deep inside... Somehow I knew that our nice life was only temporary... that it would somehow be shattered. I tried to brace for it, but I didn't know exactly how. So I did the only things I knew to do back then... I clung extra tightly to my horse as I rode bareback through the cool breeze... I chewed ever so slowly, embellishing every bite of bacon grease and beans... And I hugged my daddy especially hard, and I laughed excessively hard, during our endless conversations about life...

The next year, the Missouri schools were integrated. I remember being so excited, as I thought about learning in the same classroom as my best friend, Suzy. My hands shook uncontrollably as I put my favorite yellow bow in my hair the morning of my first day of school.

The school was a short block-and-a-half stroll from our home. Though it was close, I had never been allowed in. I would only try to peek into the windows at night. How wonderful it would be to finally glide right in as a peer!

The colors, the trophies, the banners all greeted me right inside the doorway, as I walked into the huge, clean hallways of the Cameron School. The stimulating aroma of bleached walls and floors mixed with the colognes and perfumes of the rich white kids quickened my heartbeat. I could hardly contain my eagerness as I entered the sixth-grade classroom.

The usual loud talking of students quieted, replaced by a silent staring at me as if on display. They made sure they gave me the full message that I was not only the new student, but the only black student in the classroom.

I quickly ignored the rudeness and spotted Suzy. I noticed the seat directly in front of her was open. Suzy was talking to a girl next to her, as I dropped my books on the desk in celebration, hoping she would notice me.

"Surprise!" I blurted out, watching for her reaction, waiting to see if she would acknowledge me as her closest friend.

Suddenly her eyes popped over at me like she was frightened. Then, in a quick second, she seemed aggravated at me. Her shocked expression reminded me of the lady actresses I'd seen in the horror movies while I sat in the balcony reserved for "Blacks Only" at the movie theater.

The teacher walked in and firmly said, "Everyone take a seat please."

Still confused by Suzy's strange behavior, I turned and squeezed myself into the desk.

What happened next is something that I will never forget. Every white person in the room moved to the other side of the room and quickly sat down. At first, I wondered... maybe they all received new assigned seats before I was admitted to school, but that seemed so innocent based on experience. I understand now... that that inner thought was only a thought to protect myself from harm. Many of them snickered as I noticed their unrehearsed commonality, displaying the sudden way whites treated black folks, especially when groups of them were all together.

I sat stunned and all alone. I was left in a row of desks by myself, the entire row next to me also empty as the other students stood in the back of the classroom rather than to sit next to me. The students all stared at me, some with amazement, some with hate. and some with anger, as if I had done something wrong.

And Suzy, too. She sat among them. She had a look on her face that I had never seen, aimed directly at me. Now I was her target of discontent. I was shocked. I did all I could do to control the confused look on my face towards her. Disbelieving Susie's behavior, I lowered my head onto my desk. I quickly tried to recall the wonderful days we had played under the shade tree, the times she had voiced her hope in us always remaining best friends.

All I could do was sit… in the thickness of silence. I took a deep breath, lifted my head, looked around the room and tried my best to focus on the teacher. I thought, 'Okay, when the teacher starts talking, all eyes will be off me'. But just then a spit wad came directly towards me from a sling shot.

"Put away that Nigger-shooter!" the teacher yelled.

Then he covered his mouth in the course of embarrassment. To my surprise, the teacher's use of the word nigger caused all the students to burst out laughing.

The teacher then said, "Excuse me, Betty. I forgot you were in here."

I took one last look around to confirm that I was the only black student in class.

"Suzy…" I whispered her way. It would be my final, desperate plea for our friendship...

Suzy glanced around the room, momentarily wondering what she should do. Suddenly, every student gave audience to the anticipation of her next move. Several white students smirked and leaned their bodies towards Suzy as if to ask, 'And what are you going to do about this?'

Then, without a word, Suzy composed herself, stood up, and walked over to me.

This would be her righteous stand, I thought.

Emboldened recounts of summer activism flashed through my mind. No one messed with Suzy's brother... No one messes with Suzy's friends... I braced for a smile, a speech, a loud "back off", or maybe even a hug in front of all her classmates.

Suzy stood over me for a second, did a quick flip of her blondish hair, moved her mouth in a slow, circular motion, and... I saw the spit gush out of her mouth and onto my forehead.

I was frozen with disbelief as Suzy strutted back towards her classmates. She raised a hand in victory as they laughed and howled.

Instinctively, I looked towards the teacher, a middle-aged white man with black-framed glasses. He ignored my look of distress by looking down at some notes he had written before class.

For some indescribable reason, he now seemed to gaze at me, in all my anguish, while allowing the other students to continue snickering and tossing insults.

Jubilant voices filled the room...

"That oughtta' teach her," I heard a boy squawk.

"Now she's learnin'!"

"Is she gonna cry?"

"Hope she leaves and don't come back..."

I now knew clearly the impracticality of my people's reality. There was no one that was going to stand up for anyone black... not

Suzy, not a stranger, not my parents, and not even my own teacher. The thought of any sort of popularity, joy, or acceptance in this school had been violently extracted.

My heart sank...

Now I wondered if there was any sort of humanity so that I could remain unfettered in the class. Just to sit there invisibly would have been a win, but the cruelty and silence of the teacher confirmed the worst, and my slim hopes vanished completely.

How I longed to be hidden in the thick, black smoke from the trains at my old school. Though I had been afraid, at least that darkness would eventually lift. Now I was in the open, on display... unceasingly alone like an animal in a hidden cage. This was worse... much, much worse.

It was here where my happy, color-blind childhood ended. The brutal reality that I was in a lawless country that encouraged atrocities, at least subtle, but often violent against its black citizens, hit me like a hard punch to my gut. My innocent condition vanished like a rock to the bottom of the pond where I used to swim, the only place we could swim, mindlessly... without fear. Now, suddenly, I understood what my daddy had gone through every day of his life. This was the reality of our circumstances based solely on skin tone.

At the old school, I had prayed that the dark smoke would lift. Now I prayed that the darkness would swallow me up again.

A single teardrop hit the floor as I struggled to feel accepted.

8

"Clairvoyance, Prophecy, Voodoo... Life"

The school bell rang to end the day, and I sprinted out the door. I ran out onto the dusty road where, at a little distance, I could see our property. Never had it looked so inviting before. Tears began to stream down my face, and I could barely see, as I continued sprinting, trying not to fall down. Suddenly I saw the silhouette of my daddy. He had been waiting for me, as if he knew what I was going to experience. I ran straight into his arms, as he knelt down to receive me.

"Oh, Daddy..."

But he hushed me and held me tightly in his arms. "I already know," he said softly. "I seen you in the clouds... Your head was down, and you were crying."

It was as if I didn't need to say a single word. He seemed to know everything I had gone through, and, most importantly, he understood it perfectly.

"I know," daddy whispered. Continuing to comfort me, he said, "Now hush Betty. Stop your sobbing. You don't need to say anything, I already know..."

Finally, I lifted my head, looked him straight into the eyes and said, "I don't want to go back, Daddy."

"You got to go back, Betty," he said. "You got to go to school."

"You want me to go through all that mess again, Daddy?" I screamed. "I can't..."

"You have to," Joshua said firmly. "Now that you know... You have to maneuver yourself through the system, Betty. Evil as it is, you got to learn how to come out a winner. You got to learn how to get through it all. And lesson one is that you don't quit. You stick to what is right, you endure the costs, and you don't ever quit!"

"I don't know if I can keep going," I said, the tears starting to roll again.

My daddy looked at me, as he stood back up to his feet. "It breaks my heart that y'all got to grow older seeing how ugly this world really is... It don't bother me so much when it happens to me. But when the lessons hit you... well... It just kills me when it happens to y'all..."

He looked into the sky seeming to recognize something. He smiled slightly. "But we will come out on top," he said softly. "It is already written that we will come out gloriously..."

I never knew exactly what Daddy saw in the clouds that day, nor did I know at the time what he meant by "we" when explaining who would come out on top. But I learned to trust big Daddy Joshua. And when he said that day that it was already written that we would come out gloriously, something fueled the insides of me that would never stop.

The clouds, the Lord, the songs, the faith, the Blood... or just simply the "Gift" is how we got through every day. In whatever way you want to describe it, "It" was what kept me going to school, holding my head high each day... come what may. "It" was what got me out of bed each morning, bearing the stares, the insults, the ignorant jokes, and the general mistreatment from the staff to the students. "It" was what pushed me to persevere year after year. And when I felt like I would explode and fail to survive, that next ten seconds were to remember what Daddy had said.

As we grew older, we began to behold more clearly "the gift" and how it applied to our lives. Many facets of discerning the spiritual realm were not always joyful or welcome. But this was a part of us, and we got used to it, though we never ceased to be amazed by it.

For example, my mom's brother, Uncle Tommy, reported that he had a vision one day. The Lord told him in the vision that his own son would die with his shoes on. No one knew why the Lord told him that, but no one questioned it either. All we could do was to secretly file it into our memories, waiting to see if the vision would come to pass. And we knew that someday it would.

One night, Tommy's son, Junior Randall, was in jail. He had accepted some kind of challenge to drink a fifth of whiskey for $10 but only if he could drink it in ten minutes. Junior drank the fifth in less than ten minutes and won the bet. Later that night, Junior lay down on his cot, never to get up again. When they found him dead in the morning, his shoes were still on.

My sister, Esther, woke up one night from a dream that had terrified her. She had seen a car in her dream that went careening off of a bridge. All three young men in the car, barely older than teenagers, drowned in the water. Esther saw their terrified looks, their gasping for air, their astonished eyes of fear, and, finally, their lifelessness. The very next day, we heard about those three young men, local boys, who had died when their car went off the bridge, just as Esther had seen them die the night before in her dream. One of the boys had just gotten back from the war in Vietnam.

Then there were the psychics or the clairvoyants, and palm readers that scattered the Missouri territories making a living from paying customers. We quickly learned from the festivals, carnivals, and traveling gypsies that we weren't the only ones who had "the gift". And everyone who had the gift did not, of course, use it for the love of God. After all, our family felt a psychic was simply a prophet who used the same gift for their own purposes. And using psychic energy for any other purpose than for God's messages, whether conscious or unconscious, whether intended or not, is using it for the "prince of the world" or the "dark side"... in other words, for Satanic use. We learned that the one having these gifts should only take instructions from the God of heaven and earth, and then use them for Him.

Then you have a whole slew of "prophets" who are wannabe's or liars. They are the false prophets who don't have the gift in the first place. And, after Mamma's healing, after she forced us to attend services, I noticed a whole lot of these people preaching inside the churches. Hearing from the true God began to get very confusing at times.

The voodoo doctors, mostly operating forty miles south in Kansas City, were well known among the African and Haitian cultures in those days. Their stories were well known on our porch, because a few happened to be members of our own extended family.

We had a distant aunt who went to see a voodoo doctor because she had a huge lump on the top of her foot. The story goes that the witch doctor came back with a huge knife.

"What you gonna' do with that knife?" our aunt asked.

"I'm going to cut that frog right out of your foot," he answered.

After numbing her foot with some strange concoction, he made a long incision over the lump, and a real live frog came jumping out of her foot!

Although these stories seemed far-fetched and even funny sometimes, we understood them to be real. The "gift" had taught us that evil spirits were real. Therefore, their leader, the devil himself, was real. And, therefore, his power was real. However, I would learn that later when the devil came a-calling for our whole family. I learned his power is only temporal, and those who engage in it will, sooner or later, be destroyed... usually sooner. The one thing that voodoo or black magic could not touch was those protected directly by the Lord Jesus. And that don't mean those that do evil in his name. There were plenty of "fake believers" that we heard about who found themselves under a curse or spell. Witchcraft was real. Those who faked real love toward God were unprotected prey, and the results of that could be anything.

Many well-known stories were told to us as children. You can be the judge as to whether you think it was real or not, but the stories that were told to us happened even to friends of our family.

One story was about a young man who had fallen deeply in love with a girl, but his mother didn't like her. The girl would come over the house speaking in a very arrogant and demeaning way to the mother and to the rest of his family. The girlfriend knew that the mother's son was going to marry her anyway, so she came over often and provoked his mom with teasing and laughter. Finally, the mother, being annoyed and seeking solutions, found that her son's girlfriend loved cabbage stew. And, one day, before one of her taunting visits, the mother had prepared a pot of tantalizing cabbage stew. The mother had spiced it so that the aroma was beyond inviting.

"Would you like a bowl of cabbage stew?" the mother asked the girl as she walked haughtily through the door and into the kitchen.

The girl didn't know why the mother was acting so nice, but she couldn't resist. Afterwards, the son's girlfriend got very sick and went to a voodoo doctor.

"You've been fixed on cabbage," the witch doctor reported to her.

This meant she had been poisoned by a black magic or voodoo spell that was prepared in the form of cabbage. Two days later, the girl died.

Then there was the outrageous story of the girl who couldn't get a boyfriend. Although she seemed somewhat pretty and had a wonderful personality, no one would ask her on a single date in her thirty-four years of life.

She went to one of the Kansas City sorcerers to help her.

"You have 'cow face'," the voodoo doctor said to her.

"What does that mean?" the girl asked.

The witch doctor kept a perfectly straight face as he explained his diagnosis with his broken accent. "Every time a boy see you, he see a cow."

So they performed some sort of ritual to get rid of the cow face. The story always made us laugh at the ridiculousness of the situation and the solution. However, all we know, and the way the story went, is that the very next man the girl met asked her out and ended up marrying her. And they were married until death.

Back in those days, if some of our Africans' ancestors, got mad, and went to a voodoo doctor, there was a good chance that any person being targeted by their anger would turn up dead that very next week. Voodoo witch doctors were as popular and real in African and Haitian cultures on American soil as medical doctors. After a time, no one dared question their religious significance and effectiveness. We saw the spiritual realm, both good and bad, at work constantly.

Our family was chosen by God, for whatever reason, to see things. We saw them mostly in visions and dreams. It wasn't unusual to hear one of us in the midst of the night suddenly wake up after dreaming a scene, often a dream about someone's coming death, a far-away unknown murder, or the future plans God had in store for a person we knew. We were 'Warning Prophets'. It's just the way it was. We learned to pray and go back to sleep. Whether we heard about the murder, death, or event, the next day, we had become susceptible to any occurrence. It was something that we were callous to. We had to be. We really had no choice. The dreams, the visions, the sightings, the voices… none of them were voluntary. They just were. Like the weather, they were out of our control.

There was the stranger who came by while we were on the front porch, an old Haitian lady. She stopped and told my mamma to never wear black.

"What?" Mamma asked, after hearing her perfectly well.

The woman just looked at her, knowing full well that Mamma heard her.

"Why?" Mamma finally blurted out…

The woman stood a few seconds longer before looking down and slowly walking off…

She waved her hand in the air as if throwing something at Mamma, but didn't look back. "Just don't never wear anything black," she said again, as she walked on down the road.

Only one time did I see my mamma wear a black dress after that, and that was for a funeral. That same day, Mamma got deathly sick, but recovered after about three or four days. Never again did Mamma wear black. And that was that…

Almost daily, I would hear my parents, or someone in our home, recollecting one of literally hundreds of stories that had happened to our family. A common name I heard in many of those stories was a lady named Minnie Rollaway, my daddy's aunt in St. Joseph. Minnie was a clairvoyant. When she was a little girl, she could find anything that anyone had lost. All someone had to do was to tell Millie what they lost, and she would kneel down on the floor and spit in her hand. Every single time, without fail, her spit would begin to creep a certain direction, as if it had a mind of its own. Whichever way the spit went, that's where the lost item would eventually be found.

As Minnie got older, she often used her gifts to tell folks how to get rich. Many a white person would visit Minnie, and, if she "had anything for them" from the spiritual realm, she would tell them exactly what steps to take to prosper financially. Minnie would always be right.

Later, Minnie got married. She and her husband had a fairly good-sized home. A black family with a decent-sized home was an important source of income back in those days. If a black homeowner had room, they could rent out parts of their home as a rooming house. In St. Joseph, and Missouri in general, there were always black men who worked for the trains, the railroad, or other jobs who would look for a temporary place to rent. Even preachers passing through to the next town were a very resourceful use of income. Everything back then was segregated, so a black homeowner with space could make fairly consistent money off their home just by providing a room to sleep and a hot meal.

When Daddy Joshua was younger, he walked from Cameron to St. Joseph, a 32-mile stroll, to visit Aunt Minnie. He was looking for work, and he figured Aunt Minnie might give him an answer.

"Well, you could work right here in St. Joseph," Aunt Minnie told him. "Just stay here tonight, and I'll fix you a good meal. Then, tomorrow morning, go down to the packing house. No matter what it looks like, that's where you'll get hired right away."

The next morning, Joshua woke up and headed straight to the packing house about a mile away. There were 70 to 80 strong men, many of them white, waiting in a line to be picked for work. Daddy's heart sank. But, immediately, out of the blue, a white foreman looked his way.

"You!" the man yelled, pointing straight at Joshua.

Joshua hesitated in shock.

"I want you to be a shackler," the man went on. "Come on…"

Aunt Minnie had been right again.

I'm not sure why, maybe because folks weren't always relying on electronics and material things, but the supernatural always seemed hyper-activated back then. Maybe we were always paying a whole lot more attention to it instead of our phones.

One night, Mamma went up to church with a huge lump on her hand that the older folks used to call a "baker's knot". When she got to church, her aunt Sarina, whom Mamma was named after, began to massage the lump. She didn't even greet Mamma or say a word. She sat down beside her, and she began to slowly massage the lump while holding Mamma's hand and listening to the praise choir. Within seconds, the lump and the pain were completely gone with no sign. Aunt Sarina got back up without a word. She stood, lifted a hand, praised the Lord, and nothing more was ever said about it. Strange…

From the old wives' tales and histories in the South came superstitions. If your nose was itching, it meant someone was coming. Daddy would never let anyone take a photo of him. For some reason, he was always scared that the photo would end up in a stream. And, he believed, as the photo faded, the person on it would die also. Everyone was different. Each person would latch onto the superstitions they chose and mix them with their belief system from the Holy Bible or from whatever religion they chose. They would take the combination of the two, and then mix it with personal experiences and the evidence they either wished or witnessed to be true. Like ingredients from a made-up recipe, each person's mental conviction ended up as diverse as their DNA.

Generally speaking, though, I always noticed some differences based on whether a person was black or white. Most black people always seemed to believe in something going on outside of themselves, referring to an actual Higher Power at work, while many white folks seemed to solely trust their own instincts, calling their feelings the "higher power". And you know how much trouble you can get in by doing that.

But the gift that our family had was completely different from a philosophical mindset. These entities were involuntary and real. I remember vividly seeing a beautiful black lady come to my bedside when I was a child. She had on a white gown that flowed brightly, even though it was dark in the room. "Mamma!" I yelled, thinking it was her. But then my mom came into the bedroom to see what I wanted, her clothes and image shadowed by the darkness. Mamma saw my eyes affixed to someone or something, then she calmly lay beside me, coaxed my hair, and refrained from saying a word. I watched the beautiful, glowing image of that "angel" until I slowly went back to sleep.

I listened carefully as I grew up in order to reach my own reality. What was real or what was not? I had to learn, or I felt I would go insane. But now I learned that there were two sides in the spiritual realm. And they were total opposites. The angels, the "good ones", that is... had an expression of peace, love and kindness on their faces. The bad ones always had contorted expressions of pure combativeness and anger. With the beautiful angels came an indescribably wonderful scent. With the devilish ones came a putrid smell like a sulfuric stench, far worse than any decaying animal. Many angels resonated sounds of brilliant harmony, and the other ones groaned the most vicious, guttural growls I have ever heard. I most often "felt" their presences before I even saw them! A quiet, relaxing spirit accompanied the cherubim like a sea of crystal glistening over the clear blue waters. A dark, oppressive fog of blackness covered my bedroom walls when the bad ones were present.

I learned that a sudden surge of positive energy and cheerfulness meant that a good spirit had descended upon me. Good versus evil was always at work, but the wonderful presence of the heavenly powers were hidden from the foul person and unbelieving.

The strange thing is... when evil men follow their calling they are unaware of the magnitude of the grotesque creature that dwells within.

I learned that evil deceives those who believe only in what they can see. Therefore, I began to distrust those folks or avoid them altogether.

One day, as a six-year-old, I decided to confide in the white pastor's wife and tell her about a devil I had seen.

"Oh, Betty," she cooed with unbelief in her voice. "You are just seeing bedroom monsters. They are only in your imagination. They ain't real..."

"But I saw it plainly," I argued.

"Now, Betty, then you are only just seeing things. They're not really there..."

As I grew older, and as I shared the sightings with my family, I began to see just how different we were. But something else happened as well. I began to form a confidence in myself. It was as if I held a powerful secret that most people didn't know. I feared the Lord because I had seen His creations. And the fear of the Lord, as the bible says, is the beginning of knowledge. I beheld a knowledge that most dismissed. With this knowledge, I learned to manipulate the spirits with a prayerful word because they were ever at the mercy of all those who believed that the highest Spirit of all was God. And, I figured, if I could manipulate spirits, I could have a discernment of people who were affected by those spirits. And, if my theory was correct, I could then manipulate how people treated me. Maybe?

How liberating it was to discern which spirits were working with which people, as I learned to recognize each realm by their individual expressions. After all, I had seen various kinds of angelic beings that, by their expression, indicated to me which kind had just entered into my bedroom.

As I carried out my hypothesis, I began to watch for how certain white men of the town spoke to Daddy forcefully, for example. I began to study their expressions while they were talking. They would form an outer appearance of anger and hatred which let me know the inner man was controlled by an unseen spirit. I learned to recognize these evil spirits, even when many of the men smiled at Daddy.

One day, I heard a white man yelling at Daddy outside. I looked out the window. But, instead of just looking at the man's face, I began to peer into the soul behind the face. There it was... I saw the devil inside of him! Thinking quickly, I grabbed a cupcake off the stove and ran outside.

"You're not worthy to charge us money for picking up our trash!" the man yelled. He fingered a pistol he was carrying. "I'm not gonna' watch a nigger get rich offa' my money. I'll see you in hell before I pay my hard-earned..."

Suddenly, he stopped. Neither he nor Daddy had noticed me sneaking closer, but now I was standing right next to the man that was taunting Daddy. Neither one of them had a chance to do anything. I had already placed my left hand on his hand, the same hand that was reaching for the gun. Inside, I told that devil to get away. The man's face turned calm and pale. He seemed to forget everything he was saying. I handed the cupcake to the man with my right hand, and then I ran back inside the house. He stood there silently and looked down at the chocolate cupcake I had given him. Daddy seemed equally perplexed. After a few more seconds, looking puzzled, the man just turned away and walked calmly down the street.

Daddy hurried inside and looked at me. "What are you doin', Betty?" he asked.

"I spoke to the devil," I said. "And he left!"

Daddy smiled the biggest smile. He shook his head and laughed, as he walked towards the door.

"Don't ever do that again," he added, before walking back outside.

But, I have to admit, I didn't listen to Daddy. I had learned that day how to control evil, and it wasn't something I was going to forget.

My periods of spiritual self-education were forming an understanding, a truth about all men. The kids at school and the people Daddy had to deal with, the ones who hated others for no reason... they all used to make me angry. But understanding the spirits they carried daily, plus the ones that controlled them, helped ease my hostility. I came to know that it wasn't totally people's faults or their own doing, no matter how ignorant they seemed. And ignorance can make you seem evil. This information for me sustained a type of pity I referenced towards those who violated us.

I meditated one day and applied this theory to slavery and mistreatment. I closed my eyes and imagined all the souls involved. I saw the downtrodden slaves. There they were, in my mind, working, singing, toting the bible, obeying the masters... and then there was a fast-forward as I envisioned them in heaven, smiling, singing, worshiping the true Master. And then, into focus, came the haters... money-loving, self-exalting, lying, cheating men, who used the backs of slaves to gain wealth, high living, and international prestige. I imagined them now burning in hell, tormented like the rich man in Luke 16.

They had lost all, forever...

The coming of a righteous judgment took away all of my anger...

As I grew more knowledgeable about spirits, love, hatred and life, something began to happen that I never would have suspected. There began to be more fighting in our own home. It was as if the wars from the outside had entered and made their habitation among all of us. There we were, siblings, parents, other family members... daily, growing older, and we began to turn against each other. Suddenly, it wasn't the "white outside" that attacked us. We, ourselves, began to attack one another. It was as if the front lines had reversed from the inside out. It was as if some of the family began to believe the lies that we were less human... And we now carried out our own hatred on ourselves or those in our home.

And, when we believed the lie, its aim administered itself directly at our family causing havoc within us!

Oh, Mamma and Daddy tried to resist it, but even they began to argue with one another while we destroyed each other with insults and angry looks. Diablo had contemplated and activated a new strategy. And none of us seemed to know how to reverse this unfamiliar attack from close encounters and trusted traitors.

Only one thing seemed to be going right at home... George seemed to be improving. He was actually beginning to move around pretty well, as if his body had awakened and was tired of being immobile. He still didn't say anything. He pretended not to hear the fighting as he rotated his eyes from person to person. Every once in a while he would push his glasses back upon his nose, after having lowered them when he had had enough, and wanted to make believe he was in another world.

No one even commented much on George's improvement. Everyone seemed intent on arguing. This was no longer "playing the Dozens" for fun. This was mental and emotional warfare.

At church, the next Sunday, the preacher spoke about the peace of Jesus. "Jesus came to earth to bring us peace…" For some reason, he glanced over at me where I was sitting in my usual spot near the back corner of the church. He gave me a quick frown. Then he refocused, smiled at the congregation, lifted his hands, and, like fireworks, let out another blast. "Peace on earth, and goodwill to men," he shouted. "Jesus brought us peace on earth and goodwill to all men! Let us rejoice! Thank you, Jesus, for peace! Amen and amen!"

I walked towards home that afternoon, but I stopped at the park. The day was so warm and beautiful. I lay down in the grass under a tree. Then I heard a voice.

"Betty," an angel whispered.

"What!" I blurted out. I sat up and looked around. I suspected the voice was an angel, but I looked around to make sure no one else was near. I sat still, waiting, my heart beginning to pound nervously in my chest.

"You know that's not true," the voice spoke. "What the false prophet said…"

"What!" I said again, more quietly this time.

"Yeshua came not to bring peace… but peace to some men and a sword to others. That was a lie…"

"What do you mean?" I asked. "Of course Jesus came to bring peace…"

"Shhhhhhhh," the wind whispered in the trees above.

I waited and waited. I listened intently for the voice to return. I lay back down and closed my eyes.

The angel whispered again. "Yeshua came to bring division…"

"What?" I blurted out again. "Division?"

I didn't want to go home. The fighting among the siblings had gotten worse than ever, and home didn't feel like home anymore.

The voice was now silent. I ran home to find a bible and try to find what this division stuff was all about.

I spotted a bible next to George and grabbed it without a word. I sat down at the kitchen table and read as fast as I could. Then there it was. I could hardly believe it!

"Think not that I am come to send peace on earth: I came not to send peace, but a sword..."

These words were in red! These words were from Jesus? But the angel said "Yeshua".

I remember some of the church folk as well as a few family members, called him Yeshua when praying, but the preacher at church called him Jesus. So did I. I became confused. I read on...

"Oh, there's miss Goody Two Shoes reading the bible," one of my brothers blurted out. I turned my head to avoid what was said.

I walked out of the house stunned. I went back to the park and under the tree, my bible still in my hand. I felt like I was in a trance. *Why would Jesus send a sword on the earth?* I wondered. *Why would the Son of God actually promote division? Maybe to get the good people away from the bad,* I thought...

I could feel the Spirit speaking to me as I lay down again under the tree. Then it hit me... I had learned as a child that there were only two sides... total opposites. That's what we're doing here. That's why we're here on this earth. That's why we're all living our lives that will lead up to a final judgment. We're being divided! And the sword is dividing us, and the sword is the Word of God. And Jesus was called the Word... Suddenly, it came together and made sense. We're all living our lives to be divided into two groups, the folks with a divine nature of love or the devil's folks. And we can actually choose which side we want to be on! Jesus came to die. But not to unite us, but to divide us... The right from the wrong!

I thought about my Sunday school lessons, how they talked about the weeds and the wheat, the sheep and the goats. Each had their role and each role was based on choice. This was the division.

The wind blew....

My bible fell open a few pages, and it read... "Blessed are those who hunger and thirst after righteousness for they shall be filled".

A couple of teenage boys walked by at that moment. "Hey, I didn't know niggers knew how to read," I heard one of them say, while the other one glanced over and laughed.

"I ain't a nigger!" I said. "I'm an Israelite!" The second part just came out of my mouth uncontrollably.

"A... a... um... a what?" one of the boys stuttered.

I hesitated. I wasn't confident enough to speak up on how meaningful being an Israelite was, because I really wasn't sure what that meant myself. But something inside of me, something not me, stirred an anger that wasn't really anger. It was as if something inside of me was being compelled for me... or for truth. I'm not sure what the boys saw, but they looked stupefied.

I was now sixteen years old. And I had stood up for myself, or at least something inside of me had stood up for me... I wasn't exactly sure what had happened, but I felt good. It was as if the world was coming into focus and making sense for the very first time in my life.

I slowly asserted myself back to my resting place under the tree. The bible lay on the ground. I crossed my legs to hold it in place, while the wind turned another page. There on the page I saw a picture.

It was a picture of an angel. For a minute or more, I couldn't breathe.

My soul was at peace...

The seasons changed in their dramatic Missouri fashion, and the fighting in our home seemed to get worse and worse. I could actually see the two divisions, and the spiritual strategies taking place that caused those divisions. At one point, my little brother Ephraim shouted out the "nigger" word. I was astounded!

I imagined myself grabbing his throat and telling him, 'Don't ever say that again.'

I kicked him instead.

"Mom!" he shouted and ran.

9

"Wished In Death"

It was now the Fall of 1950. And, while the contentions continued on in our crowded home, something horrible and revealing appeared right outside our front door... A psychic came by. This wasn't really unusual. Many witches, gypsies, and psychics would travel through Cameron before heading off to the next town. But this psychic was different.

She stood in front of our home, a skinny, white woman, but much paler than most... a stranger with big, fearful eyes. I could sense the witchcraft spirit of darkness all around her, which matched her black apparel.

The wind blew the leaves, as she stood like a statue in front of our home. My siblings and I stopped playing and quit arguing. A few of us sensed, but we all noticed, her gloomy presence. Family members visiting inside the house as well as those outside, sensed the morbid reality of her presence. Some of them just heeded to natural curiosity, peeking out the window, and others came out to gather around her like an audience waiting to hear something exciting. My daddy came from around back from feeding the chickens. Sensing an evil presence, he stopped for a moment and stood next to my mother. He had a stern, look upon his face as he approached the enchantress.

An evil grin formed on her face as Daddy came closer. Mamma stayed back, clutching a broom in her hands. Nervous about the presence of her appearance, Mamma motioned for me to come and stand next to her.

"I have... something... to... tell you," she said slowly, her gaze transfixed onto Daddy. "I've come a long, long way to tell you... something…"

Daddy was not intimidated. "Well, speak on," he commanded with a quick nod.

She looked at the home, then at us kids circled around Mamma, and then back at Daddy. She could sense "the gift" in many of us, and she feared us. Somehow I just knew it. She glanced nervously my way, and then quickly back at Daddy.

"I need s-s-silver," she said with a hiss.

"Oh, we don't have any money," Mamma quickly spoke up. But she stayed back.

Daddy seemed to anticipate the request. He impatiently reached into his pants pocket, produced a fifty-cent piece, and tossed it into her bony, pale hands.

"Go ahead, ma'am," he said nervously. "Speak on now!"

The woman gave another wicked grin, while placing the money into a raggedy black purse. She seemed to wait, gesturing for a few more coins, but Daddy would have none of it.

"I said speak on now or give me back my coin," he said rudely.

The woman leaned towards him before speaking. "Wished in death!" she whispered loudly.

Everyone stood there in disbelief that she would give such a dreadful seance. Her eyes squinted, and she seemed slightly annoyed that no one showed any fear… or any other reaction, for that matter.

"Wished in death!" she repeated, slightly louder.

Again, no reaction.

"You have a curse on you, on all of you. One of you will go blind, and another will lose their mind!"

She stepped back a couple of steps and looked up at the house. "Oh, this home," she stammered. "This home is also wished in death!" By now she had raised her voice to a level that frightened me. I wanted to knock that devil right out of her, but I couldn't move...

Daddy stood there without saying a word. She seemed annoyed that we were so quiet. She looked at Daddy, then again at Mamma, as if she was trying to convince them of the seriousness of her message.

"You've all been cursed, and your home is wished in death!" she screamed one last time. And then she turned, seemingly with disappointment, and swiftly walked away.

Mamma seemed concerned, even a bit startled, but Daddy just gave a slight smirk, waved a hand, and went back around to continue working and feeding the animals. Not a word was said about it afterwards.

I didn't know what 'wished in death' would really mean for our family, but I knew that blackness filled the air. I felt the evil, and I knew that something had just happened that wasn't good. I saw a storm ascending over the horizon. Darkness appeared as the sun disappeared into the clouds. Leaves bounced into the wind between the freshly harvested fields. Mamma lowered her head and went into the house. Daddy was in the back, muttering something, but he went right on working.

Everyone dispersed and went back to what they were doing. Only me and George were left standing, watching the woman as her silhouette disappeared into the evening wane.

George moved slowly with pain as if he was hurting. For months now, George had been better, making great progress... going outside, managing himself, eating his own meals, watching all the arguments…

But, this moment, he slumped to one knee and put his head into his hands.

Then he slowly looked up at me to see if I had noticed.

10

"George's Death... and Mine"

As I grew older, I noticed that men began to look at me differently. Men with their wives and families in the store would sneak a look at me, form a sly perching of their mouth, look down first, quickly glance at my lower body parts, before their eyes made their way back up to mine. Then a little smirk or a tip of their hat followed just before anyone else noticed. The timing was impeccable, the gesture unmistakable... a seductive evil visible , yet invisible to most...

Even some of the boys at school were treating me differently, much nicer. It's amazing what hormones can do for race relations...

Not long after the witch's warning, George's health began to decline rapidly. Even on that day, he returned into the house, never to come outside again. His progress had reversed, and now he continually stayed in bed. Soon he barely moved, as if paralyzed. George, left dumb by the accident, still couldn't speak, but now he moaned and rolled his head uncontrollably, confused, and in agony.

After a few months, George's eyesight completely went, and then he just lay in bed in a catatonic stupor. His eyes, though in darkness, seemed to stare up at the ceiling wide open. I could see the pain and anguish that it caused my mamma and daddy as they fed him and called the doctors. But no one knew what to do. The doctors blamed a blood clot on his brain. If that were the case, it probably had been there since the day he had said that he was kicked by the horse.

I recalled the words of the witch that spoke the curse... One will be blind, and another will lose their mind and go insane.

Two things confused me... First, I couldn't seem to break this curse with my prayers. And, second, why did it seem that both curses had settled on poor George?

By now, Dan and Esther, were in middle school. June, the talkative one, and Lawrence were right behind them in grade school. Joshua, Jr. was slightly less than a year behind Lawrence. And the baby was now Everett Francis, better known as Butchy.

I remember little Butchy, barely able to walk, going over to George and kissing him on his face. George could only stare at the ceiling, unable to wipe off the slobber. The toddler was oblivious to the message that he was carrying. George seemed to sense the love from this tiny messenger, though he couldn't react to it. Somehow I knew that George had felt that kiss, that attention, from God Himself. It was as if the angels were gathering again for a homecoming. The simple kiss seemed to tell George, "Hold on, my son. It won't be long. Your long, hard, misunderstood life is nearly fulfilled."

After Butchy would kiss him and run away smiling, I saw George's fingers doing some crazy movements at the side of the bed. No one else noticed. But, every single time someone kissed George, changed his bedpan, fed him, or did something nice, even comb his hair, I noticed the movements with his fingers. There was a certain pattern to the movements...

What in the world was George doing? I watched this for days before it suddenly hit me. Was George doing sign language? Was George communicating to us with his fingers?

I went to the school library the next day. It bothered me a little, but I knew I would be harassed if I tried to check out a book like the white students. So, after finding a signing book, I stuck it under my blouse and walked out.

I went straight home, sat down beside George, and began my experiment. I kissed George on his forehead and watched. His fingers began moving around. They moved so fast, it was impossible for me to follow. I kissed him again. The same pattern of rapid finger movements overwhelmed me. I kissed him a third time, and this time I grabbed his hand quickly, holding the first finger movement in place...

His thumb was tucked between his index and middle fingers. That was my first mission... What did that mean? I studied the basic signs and saw that it meant "bathroom", "toilet", or "I have to go to the bathroom".

Did George have to go to the bathroom each time someone kissed him? That didn't make sense. I remembered that several other finger gestures followed. I kissed George again. This time, I held his hand still after the second movement... Two fingers, his index and his middle finger, pointed to the side, together. I, again, read the sign motions from the book. I found that similar sign for "horse".

"Hmmm," I whispered to myself. "Bathroom, horse?"

It didn't make sense to me yet, and George couldn't show any response to my mystery, other than rapidly tapping his index and middle fingers on his thumb. I quickly found that this meant "no".

"No?" I said loudly.

It seemed George was getting excited as he rapidly shook his fist in a forward motion. There it was in the book... "Yes..." The quick shaking of the fist meant 'yes'!

I continued to leaf through the pages of the book. At the beginning, I saw the finger signs for the alphabet. I saw George's first two gestures! Was George spelling something to us?

I continued my experiment... I kissed George again and again, and I saw the same exact patterns with his fingers each time.

After each finger motion, I held it, looked up the letter sign, and then wrote it down. When I was done, I cried uncontrollably.

"T-H-A-N-K Y-O-U", it read.

George had been using sign language for months, maybe even years, with no one noticing. We had all been far too busy fighting, arguing, and doing our own thing. Now, with George unable to move, almost completely paralyzed again, I knew that it meant the world to him that he was able to be heard. As far as I knew, George could hear us just fine. But, for George, and especially for George, being heard was important. Heck, very few stopped to listen to him, even when he could speak. And, if it wasn't for little Butchy, there were very few times when someone stopped to love him, other than Mamma, or someone getting his everyday necessities.

Genius George was still in there. He wasn't insane or a vegetable. George was just as smart as ever! Along with all his other knowledge, he had learned how to gesture signs for things he wanted or feelings he wanted people to know. But he had been ignored. Strange how the old George had only stated facts, but this new version of George seemed intent on expressing his emotions. How painful the last few months must have been for George, as he moved his fingers, and no one took notice.

I looked up the finger signs and I formed them with George's fingers until I had finished my message, "I L-O-V-E Y-O-U".

I looked for George's reaction. A tear rolled sideways from his eye as he shook his fist tightly. He understood me! And, much more importantly, he knew that I knew what he was doing. I ran as fast as I could to find Mamma. I found her outside doing laundry.

"Mamma!" I yelled from the front porch. "I understand George... I understand George!"

Mamma stopped and looked at me. It had been years since she heard George's voice. She was the one who would sit beside him, long into the night, and sing to him, read the bible to him, or just talk to him. I knew that it was Mamma who missed hearing George speak most.

"What, girl?" she asked. "George can't speak…" But I saw her anticipatory expression inner hope.

"No, Mamma… He uses sign language… He spells stuff out with his fingers…"

I could tell that Mamma was a little disappointed with that report. Unexcited, she followed me inside, not even bothering to drop a towel she had just folded. She saw the sign language book sitting on the floor and gave me one of those looks as if to say, 'I know you didn't buy that, Betty'. But that wasn't important right now.

"Say something, Mamma," I encouraged. "And I'll tell you what he says back…"

Mama still looked a little doubtful, but then she saw George shaking his fist rapidly.

"What does that mean?" Mamma asked.

"It means 'yes'. George wants to speak to you… Go ahead, Mamma…" I held the book, ready to translate.

She sat down, looking at George. She seemed so tired. It seemed she wanted to do so many things for George. So badly she wanted things to be different. She couldn't express her whole heart into words. Mamma sat silently , wondering how George knew this. Tears formed in her eyes. She took, what was a folded towel, and lifted it to her eyes, and cried.

I pulled up a chair and waited with my book ready to help.

"I…" she finally spoke, still unsure what to say or what to ask George. "I… um… George… are you… um… in pain at all?"

Whether George was lying or not, I don't know. But he tapped his fingers on top of his thumb, rapidly, over and over.

"That means 'no', Mamma," I said, proud of my sudden translation skills.

The tears ran down Mamma's dark, worn cheeks. I suddenly noticed how old and tired Mamma looked at that moment. I had never noticed that before. And I studied her as she studied George, thinking of what to say next...

All those years, Mamma had cared for him, since George first struggled with rickets, and then the horse's kick... All those years, she changed his clothes, washed him, combed his hair, sang to him... Now watching him with the same expression as a mother holding her tiny infant.

Mamma took a deep breath and spoke ever so sweetly, "I... I love you, my smart baby boy."

George shook his fist and then did another sign. He had his three middle fingers down with only the thumb and little finger up. I rapidly turned the pages of the book looking for that gesture. I found it on page five.

"Oh, that means 'I love you'. I guess that's a shortcut instead of spelling it."

George confirmed my translation by shaking his fist rapidly again. Then he began to move his fingers, waiting for me to catch up. He held his fingers in a position and waited until I said it. He was spelling something now.

"I love you?" I kept asking. But George kept tapping his fingers for 'no'. He straightened his hand and moved it in a cutting fashion to sign that he wanted to start over again.

I went back into the alphabet. There it was in letter form... 'y'.

"Y?" I asked.

George shook his fist for the affirmative. I wrote each letter down, as George slowly spelled out what he wanted to say to mama. Finally, he rested after he was done, rolling his head as if exhausted. Mama just waited for him patiently, happy that he could express himself. I read the message out loud, trying my best not to cry.

"Y-O-U... W-E-R-E... A-L-W-A-Y-S... A... G-O-O-D... M-O-M... T-O... M-E..."

Mamma just sat there a minute. She, herself, seemed more exhausted than George. Tears dripped down as she sat totally still. Then Mamma Sarina simply put her head on George's chest. She sobbed bitterly for several minutes. No one noticed that Daddy had walked in.

"Is he dead?" Daddy asked. "What's goin' on?"

"No, Daddy," I said. "George is talking to us in sign language..."

George heard Daddy's voice and began to sign letters again with his fingers, as Mamma continued to shed tears. I took notation again, only paying attention to George's left hand as he spelled something for Daddy. With each letter signed, George held it, until I spoke the letter out loud in order that he could speak.

"I... A-M... A... M-A-N," I told Daddy, after George was finished.

More times than I could count, Daddy had told George, "You need to be a man," as George seemed more interested in reading, studying, and doing experiments than in working. I know it frustrated Daddy greatly, as Mamma always came to George's defense, telling Joshua to leave him alone. Daddy would end up shaking his head, going back to his countless chores...

Daddy pulled a chair closer to sit next to George and waited. He looked at Mamma and thought about all the times she had advocated for George. After a minute or so Daddy said, "Yes, you are a man, son..."

I saw Daddy's eyes began to water. He brushed away a sudden tear and studied George with the same expression that Mamma had minutes prior. Daddy, too, looked old now... and I didn't know if old Joshua's expression was one of tiredness or regret. Daddy rarely spoke to George, even before George was bedridden. Daddy was always running around working. Now all he could do was stare, searching for the words that were hidden deep within his heart... maybe the words he had wanted to say all along to George...

"You... you are a much, much better man than me," Daddy said with a tender whisper.

George made the sign for 'no', but Daddy quickly grabbed his hand and kissed the top of it as he held it.

"You are a better man than me," Daddy said again. "I'm proud of you, son..."

Daddy swiped another kiss across George's hand, before kissing him on his forehead. Then carefully walked out the room.

A couple of days later, on a dark Friday afternoon, George would die at 27 years of age.

It was on a winter day, on one of those afternoons where the sun goes down before supper. I had been called a 'nigger' again by several kids after school. It was one of those afternoons where, after feeling sorry for myself, I walked around in the woods, not wanting to go home. I was too overwhelmed with grief to speak to God. I continued to walk and walk around the woods, disgruntled, too weary to even talk to myself.

Now I came into the house, only to see Mamma seated beside George's body, her hands brushing lightly over his face. George's eyes stared at the ceiling, lifeless. His mouth was frozen, slightly open. I knew he was gone. For some reason, Mamma was the only one there. Just silence... a few candles burning in the early night, Mamma, and... George.

"Go be with God," I heard Mamma whisper.

I tried to think of what to say to Mamma. I just stood there. I was still angry from being called a 'nigger', and now I missed out on being with George in his final moments. There were things I wanted to say to George, but now it was too late. For whatever reason, missing George's death, due to my own debauchery, made me exasperated rather than sad. It made me hate the white bullies so much more... It was their fault, too. Besides touting something as stupid as racism, they had made me miss my own brother's death... Forever, that moment was gone. Oh, how I hated that moment, mixed with a whole bunch of other feelings that I couldn't identify. It was all too much to handle. I'm not even sure Mamma knew I was there. I turned and silently walked out the door barely dodging a couple of faces from unidentified relatives who were already bringing food.

All I could do was run... And cry...

I ran into the dark fields and away from the lights. I felt the cold wetness on my cheeks. After about a mile, I stopped. Someone was burning in the distance. Probably some farmer was burning his leaves and fallen timber. I walked a good distance around the fire to stay off their property. But, as I drew nearer, I saw that this was no normal fire. Several men were gathered around a burning cross! Though I was a fair distance away, I could see the long, white robes of the KKK. One of them shouted something to the others. Although I noticed their pointed white hoods with hollowed out eyes, I had no desire to get closer to know what they were saying. I felt sickened and frightened at the same time. I heard background voices followed by loud whoops of yelling, as a couple of the men fired rounds of gunfire into the air.

At that moment, I felt the most dismal bout of hopelessness and depression that I had ever felt in my life. Everywhere I went, there was hatred and confusion... at school, at home where my brother lay freshly dead, the only momentary "cease fire" from all the bickering and turmoil of ranting family members. And now, even walking though the nature of the Lord's beauty in the surrounding fields of the town, usually my only place of hope, comfort and serenity... Men dressed for hate... Hatred for me! Now there was nowhere to go, not even a place for a temporal rest.

Was there anywhere on earth where hate didn't rule? I had no haven. I had no peace.

I dropped my knees onto the ground. "Where are you, Lord?" I asked. It seemed I had never been this desperate. "Please, God, where are you now? I need you..."

I stood and felt myself running again, even more oblivious than before into the darkness of an unsympathetic world. I ran towards the railroad tracks. Why? I had no idea... the tracks always scared me at night. But somehow, tonight, they brought me an unfamiliar solace. Out of breath, I put my body across the cold steal tracks. I could hear a train at a distance. Was it coming or going? I wasn't sure. But I had the strong enticement to jump up on one of the cars and ride it forever. Never stopping. Far away from this place. The coming train suddenly felt like an only friend. A source of consistency that had no antagonism. It blindly, dutifully, and obediently rolled on its never-changing track. The train, a source to somewhere else, an escape. And an escape seemed my only option on this dreary night. The thought of riding somewhere to another space, separated from the intensifying resentment for who God made me to be, and George's death, too, brought me sudden assurance and comfort.

Just then, flakes of snow fell silently out of the night sky. "Just great," I muttered. "Just what I need..." But the blackness of the sky became visibly brighter, as the beautiful flakes fell all around me. After the train passed by, the world around me filled again with total silence...

At that moment, I felt peace.

Daddy had told me, during one of our seemingly pointless talks, that every snowflake was different. "Thousands, millions, zillions of single snowflakes, and not one of them alike," I heard his voice echo in my mind. "Everything God makes is unique... totally different. That includes you and me, Betty Bug. We just never get close enough to see how unique each one is..." I now guessed that Daddy was talking more about people than flakes with that last observation, and I guess his talks weren't so pointless after all... Everything Daddy said seemed to have a lesson in there somewhere...

I now walked along the railways of the track; my arms stretched wide for balance. Various flakes floated around me sparkling to keep me company. Somehow my anger slowly faded away, swept into the glistening of the snowfall, until it came to a total sensation...

Free of disturbance... Free of hatred...

I walked and walked; caught in a web of unexpected tranquility that I didn't want to end. I didn't even feel cold, just a strange warmth and strength that the elements couldn't challenge.

Then I saw a different fire in the distance. A much smaller one than before. As I drew closer, making sure to be completely silent, my curiosity taunted me, pushing me closer. While I crept forward, I could see the outline of a single person hunched towards the flames. He had a dark hood over his head, much different from the white hoods I had seen earlier that night. I could hear low muttering from him saying something...

Sensing someone getting closer, just then, a small dog jumped up from the other side of him.

"Who dat?" the man asked. Standing up, and now looking my way, while the dog yapped a few quick warnings.

For some odd reason, I wasn't scared or hesitant. I walked towards the man, phasing into the moonlight...

"Hi, mister," I said, trying my best to seem cordial and not strange. "I didn't mean to scare you. I was just out here taking a walk."

The man looked at me, his face protruding from under the hood. He was an older black man with a gray beard. Something in his eyes looked tired like Daddy's.

"Mighty strange place to be taking a stroll," he said calmly, with a hint of suspicion.

"Yeah," I said quietly. I looked down at his little dog that looked back at me. Panting with excitement, she wagged her tail resiliently. I looked into the fire. I stared down at it, as my words of desperation began to pour out.

"My brother just died... and I got called a 'nigger' again today... and my parents usually fight and argue, along with the other people in my house... and I just had to leave... and I saw a Klan rally... and..."

I knew that none of these things were making sense. *He must think I'm crazy*, I thought, as I suddenly looked over at him. But he had the strangest, expression on his face, as if he understood everything perfectly.

The man shuffled his feet a little, sat on the ground, and then stretched his legs, resting them across the log he had been sitting on.

"Well, you're welcome to warm up over here," he said with a deep voice. His voice was hospitable. It wasn't like the other hobos or vagrants I had seen wander into town or camping along these tracks. No, he spoke with a sense of hidden knowledge... "And, if you're hungry, me and ol' Trixie here are having hot dogs and beans tonight. Got plenty if you're hungry…"

His dog seated herself beside him. Trixie looked in my direction as though she wanted company and seemingly begged me to stay. As the man poured a can of beans in a frying pan, I sat down on the ground the opposite side of the low flames. The fire felt so warm. I continued to stare into its mesmerizing effects.

"I'm not really hungry," I finally said. "Is it okay if I stay here awhile, though?"

"You can stay here as long as you wish, young lady," the man said, balancing the beans on a tripod he had set up over the flames. "Me and Trixie just sit here and talk. We don't sleep much anyway… It's good to have the company…"

"My name's Betty," I said. It was as if I knew the man. And, for some unknown reason, the man seemed completely safe, even trusting.

"It's nice to meet you," he said with a friendly smile. His teeth were not yellow and worn like the other men who jumped trains. His teeth were pretty and white. "You already know Trixie here… My name's Henry… Henry Ridge."

We exchanged a bit of small talk for a while as Henry fixed the hot dogs and beans. He cut up the meat into the beans and stirred them. They gave such a wonderful aroma. I secretly hoped he would fix some for me. As if he read my mind, he found a rugged but clean plate from his small tent, turned several heaping spoons, and handed it to me. A fancy restaurant would not have been more luxurious at the moment.

"Thank you," I said.

Trixie gave me a look of surprise, but Henry quietly said, "Guests first," before giving her a bowlful.

This was an amazingly delicious meal. After eating quietly, the snow stopped falling. Henry took my plate. "More?" he asked. "Got plenty!"

"No, thank you," I answered graciously, though I could have eaten three more helpings.

Again, Henry seemed to read my mind. Bent over, he reached and gave me another large helping. With a smile, I took it without hesitation. Henry sat back down, stared into the fire, and then looked at me intensely.

"I'm real sorry about your brother," he said softly. He went back to looking into the fire. "How did he die?"

For just a little while, and in spite of all that made sense, I had forgotten about George. Staring into the fire along with Henry, I began to cry. I rambled about George, his wit and intelligence, his early rickets, how he must've gotten kicked by a horse, and, finally, how he seemed to be a victim of psychic words that had been spoken right in the presence of our family.

Henry not only listened, he seemed to analyze my words, as though he was putting together some kind of case. "Where you live?" he asked.

"Here in Cameron."

"Who's yo' daddy?"

"Joshua Jackson."

Then I saw Henry smile. "I know yo' daddy... He's a good man..."

Without saying anything more, Henry turned his face in the other direction. As he looked back my way again, he breathed deeply.

"You are not a nigger," he said firmly. He had a stern but concerned frown on his face with one eyebrow lifted.

"I know," I responded.

"What else do you know 'bout yourself, young lady?" he asked.

"I know that I'm just as smart as those white kids in my class, even though the teacher don't think so…"

"That's right," Henry agreed. "And it's what *you* know that counts…"

It felt good to talk to someone new about the things that had been bothering me. I put my plate down and knelt closer to the fire. I felt so relaxed and comfortable.

"What else do you know 'bout yourself?" Henry pressed on.

I sat quietly, not knowing where he wanted to go with this amiable interrogation.

"Do you know that you're an Israelite?" he asked after a few moments. "Do you know that you're from God's chosen People?"

"Yes!" I blurted out.

Henry looked at me with surprise. "Yes?" he asked.

"Yes," I repeated. "An angel told me… in a dream…"

"You must be pretty special…" he said with a smile. "… that God Himself would send an angel to tell you that!"

"I guess I am…" I had never thought about it much. But now the dreams, the People, the drums… they all came rushing back into my mind. "But… but… I don't really know what that really… means," I stammered.

Henry had a look of kinship on his face. "I guess that's why God sent you here," he said.

Over the next hour, Henry taught me with an uncanny clarity how God's first People on earth were people of color, how they lived long ago in Israel, and how they migrated to Egypt, to the Saharan desert regions, and finally down into the West coast of Africa. He taught me how the black Israelites were put into bondage in various lands… in Assyria, in Egypt, in Babylon, in Rome, and then in

America. He told me how we were drawn out of our lands when Joseph and his brothers left in the time of famine. While others remained or went back, he taught me how Yeshua Himself had told them to "flee to the mountains" when trouble came. Henry taught me how they had kept migrating down to the Ivory Coast of West Africa in that time, and that more bondage would come when the Roman armies followed…"

"You talking about the slaves?" I asked. "Like my great grandfather?"

Henry got up and went into his tent. He came back out with a bible.

"Read this," he told me, sitting right beside me. I read what he was pointing at.

"And the Lord shall bring thee into Egypt again with ships…"

"That's the transatlantic slave trade right there," he said. "That's how us Israelites came into America."

"I thought we were African people…"

"Israel people are African people," he said. "You see, two thousand years ago Israel was part of Africa. Most people living there at that time were people like you and me. That was our homeland."

"So Abraham, Isaac, Jacob…" I tried to remember all the names of God's people. "… Joseph… you mean that they were all…"

Henry beamed at my new revelation. "… Black and brown people?"

"They were all black?" I asked with astonishment.

"It is a historical fact," Henry said, knowing that I was a quick learner. He stirred the fire's coals, as the flames shot up again. "All God's chosen, the twelve tribes of Israel, the Jews, the Hebrews, whatever group you want to call them… Moses, David, all the prophets... all the way down to the disciples... the main characters in the bible... Paul... yes, and Yeshua."

"Jesus?" I blurted out.

"Yeshua," he replied.

I recalled the lesson the pastor's wife had shown me... that one of the wise men was black, but everyone else at Christ's birth was white.

"John the Revelator saw him," he softly said. "Ol' John saw him sitting on His throne in Revelations IV... John said that He looked like jasper and sardine stones..." Henry pointed towards me. "You are a young woman, and you know your stones, don't you? What does a jasper or sardine look like?"

I didn't know my stones very well, so I pretended to understand what Henry was saying.

"It is a historical and biblical fact," Henry explained.

He had that same look. That same expression the angel had in my dream. With his face shining from the fire's glow, he explained... "Jesus is black... well, brown actually. John the Revelator said that his feet looked like burnt brass. And he had hair like wool... That man you see in today's pictures, I don't know who he is."

Henry went on talking to his new student, as Trixie laid down to sleep. But I wasn't really listening any longer. All I could think about was Jesus... now a man with a color like me. I pictured Him in my mind... walking on the water, preaching on the hillsides, hanging on the cross. This seemed so different. It seemed so right. It made sense... *No wonder everybody hates black people*, I thought. Jesus said they would hate *Him first*!

"Why do people seem to hate black people so much here?" I pondered, mostly towards myself. I was thinking about the harshness I tried to ignore every day at school.

Henry looked at me as though he seemed to know everything that I was going through. "It's spiritual," he simply answered. "Why do you think no one seems to care about the deaths of our people who are murdered?"

I recalled hearing Daddy speak of Uncle Joshua, how he was killed in jail, how it was covered... and how no one even knew about it from the newspapers... But when a white man dies, there's news, reports, investigations... conversations... grief...

"We know all about 'ol Adolf Hitler and who he killed..." Henry went on. "But did you ever learn in school that the slave trade of blacks killed more men, women, and children than the Holocaust, the Crusades, and the Inquisitions all together?"

I wasn't sure what Henry was talking about, but I respectfully listened. He stirred the embers with a hint of agitation. "We mourn the deaths of soldiers in that long Civil War," he grumbled reflectively. "And rightfully so... But no one seems to know that thirty times more people died in the Transatlantic Slave Trade... Thirty times more!" He looked at me intensely. Fighting back his emotions he said, "And why don't anyone mourn them? Why doesn't anyone mourn them with memorials, and statues, and stories, and reenactments like we do for others? Because the world doesn't feel for us. All those dead folks dumped in the ocean, in swamps, in shallow graves... tormented, in bondage to their enemies, long forgotten... like the scriptures said they would be... no-count-to-the-world, a forgotten people... without a single memorial."

Henry looked up at the sky. Traces of random flakes fell into the fire. He smiled and nodded softly. "Black Israelites, Betty... just like you and me. But we sure do count to God, because we're His! And, if we obey, the next Kingdom's going to be far different!"

I didn't want to offend Henry with my ignorance, but I had to know... And this man, Henry, seemed to be the only one around who could answer my desire to learn everything. "So all these folks we study in the bible… are…"

"Black," Henry answered, knowing where I was going. "Almost every significant person in the bible was a person of color," he repeated. "In fact, God's Word was written for a People. A people chosen. The truth is that it solely addresses his People all the way through." He raised his eyebrow once more just before finishing. "And yes, Betty, all of them looked like us ."

I let out a quick, "Uh-huh!"

Trixie raised her head up to see what was wrong.

"How do you know that these people were all black? I mean, I know John the Revelator saw Him. But…"

"You ever see pictures at your school of the Egyptian artwork they found?" Henry asked. "Your class teachers ever show you those?"

"Yes," I lied. But I knew I had seen them only in the library while searching on my own.

"What color were they?"

"They had black hair, big white eyes, and they were… brown," I said. I could see them in my memory. "Some of them carried spears… some were sitting on thrones… but, yeah, they were all brown people."

"Good," Henry said delightfully. "You are right. But did you know that they confused Joseph and Moses with Egyptians? Did you know that they confused Paul with being from Egypt?"

"No," I said slowly.

Henry showed me the stories from the bible. He read them, one by one, slowly, patiently. When he was finished, he asked me, "Now why would they confuse a white man with being a brown man? Unless they were truly…"

"Brown," I said, finishing his sentence.

Henry had a satisfied look on his face, as if he understood that his time and efforts had been well spent. "Why would a perfect bible be wrong about the color of burnt brass?"

The fire was now glowing reddish embers. Trixie was breathing heavily while Henry looked at his watch. I thought it also strange that this particular man who lived like a traveling hobo had a wristwatch on... and it seemed to be a nice one at that...

"You'd best be getting' on home," Henry said. "It's almost midnight, and I know you got a family that's probably worried to death about you, wondering where you are."

I wasn't anxious to leave, but I stood up, my backside sore from sitting so long. I shook hands with Henry, knowing that I had a long walk home. He told me to come back anytime and warned me to be careful going home. He even offered to walk me home, but I politely told him that no one knows these woods as well as me.

I walked up the hill and towards home, the glistening snow lighting the way, brightening the sky from the shadows formed, flowing against the night air.

After a few miles, I saw the streetlights of Cameron that led me to the front door of my house. There was Mamma standing on the porch and holding something. She saw me coming at a distance.

"Where you been, young lady?" she shrieked. "Your brother is dead, and you want to send me to my grave, too?"

I started to explain, but Mamma didn't seem interested.

"Here's a plate of food, Betty. It's probably cold by now. Come on inside and get in bed..."

I sat down quietly and started picking at my food. Then I noticed that Mamma was by herself and everyone else in bed. I glanced over to where George always lay. There he still was; his body covered by a white sheet.

A warm heat blazed over the fireplace, as Mamma moved rhythmically in her rocking chair. She stared into the fire just as Henry had. She didn't say anything. After a while, she began crying... at first slowly, and then without control.

"My baby," she sobbed. "My baby's gone..."

As she cried, suddenly her rocking intensified. And, as her rocking increased, so did her crying. I didn't know what to do.

I got up and knelt down beside her chair. Still holding the plate in my hand, I softly placed my right hand on her shoulder. As I pressed and squeezed, her rocking slowed.

"Did George say anything at the end Mamma?" I asked. I was curious to know since I had run away so upset, earlier.

"It was a miracle..." she whispered. "George was doing all that stuff with his fingers... And I didn't know what he was saying... But then he just began to talk with his mouth..."

"George talked?"

I waited for Mama to continue, as she wiped the tears from her face. Gasping for air, she started trying to recall the story.

Delicately she said, "... yes..."

"Yes!" She stopped rocking completely now and stared into the fire again. "George spoke again," she said forcefully. "I couldn't believe it..."

"Well, what did he say, Mamma?" I tried to keep from getting too loud or excited.

Tears recommenced as Mamma spoke.

"You know your brother," she whispered. "He told me he saw heaven, and gates, and angels... and... and all kinds of things I can't even remember… It was a miracle…" She inhaled slowly. "But then he let out one last, long breath… and he left… he just left…"

Stressed from telling the story, Mamma began sobbing uncontrollably once more. I gave her a big hug and squeezed her arm this time to let her know how much I loved her and how much I would miss George.

She closed her eyes. After a few seconds, she opened them again, and looked up at me and said, "He said…"

She seemed to be searching for the right words. "George… oh... he said… he said... said that he saw Jesus…"

I was afraid to speak, but I finally asked what was on my mind. "What did he say about Jesus?" I whispered. I was hoping to get her to refocus and tell me what he said. "Did George say what He looked like?"

"That's just it," Mamma said. "He said he saw Jesus, but he didn't make no sense…"

"Did he say what He looked like?" I pressed. "What exactly did George say?"

Mamma slowly turned towards me. The look on her face reminded me of the day George had looked at me after hearing the words from that lady in black... that skinny, white women that wished us to death.

"He said…" Mamma seemed to struggle. "George said… that Jesus was… dressed as a king." She hesitated as if not wanting to say more. I nodded for her to go on. "George said that Jesus was a noble king who was... the same exact complexion as himself!"

All I could do was stare at Mamma. The crash from my plate hitting the floor let Mamma know how shocked I was. Mamma didn't say another word. She turned back towards the fire again…

Weeping and rocking… weeping and rocking...

I swept the broken pieces up from the floor and walked softly into my bedroom. There were more bodies than normal sleeping on my bed, so I knew that family guests had stayed the night due to George's death.

I spotted a wadded-up blanket in the corner of the room, grabbed it, and lay on the floor. I envisioned my Jesus again for a while, but then my thoughts returned to George. Not many people knew the George that I knew. My brother, the intelligent charisma, the beautiful handwriting... I cried because George was gone. But I also cried because of what George had lived through, his talents and potential taken from him, leaving him only to exist, suffering to the end. The little boy. The ridicule. The prejudice of one's skin color. The heartache of living in a world of race-fill hatred. And now he joins... the dead!

I still didn't understand the total purpose of George's hard, seemingly empty, life.

'Why, Lord?' I wondered, as I closed my eyes and thought about my brother. 'Why were all his best attributes taken from him? Why was he left with only his crippled body and babbling speech? Why was he left blind, that is, until he saw heaven? What purpose did he serve?'

My stomach began to knot as I juggled feelings of anger, confusion, self- pity... and then the irredeemable... Regret.

I kept my eyes closed until my tears began to burn.

Before long, I fell into a deep sleep.

I had a dream that possessed my mind that night, and it seemed that my body was actually there, too.

I walked into a sunlit field, where a slave was working. Sweat gleamed off of his forehead, as tiny mountains of scars protruded from his slumped back. Whipped freshly, I noticed now that he had stopped working and looked up at me. And, like a baby deer whose doe had suddenly stopped feeding, another head popped up over the field of cotton ... black men, women, and children... all slaving in the hot sun.

It was like I had traveled through time, and we actually understood one other! I could feel the heat. Some of the older slaves seemed permanently hunched over. They squinted at me, as if wondering who I was. Their eyes were sad. Yet deep. I could hear a hymn, a negro spiritual, being sung in the distance. Like the faces of the innocent laborers, the song transcended into a mixture of sorrow and acclamation at the same time.

I was angry, my heart breaking, as I watched, one by one, the slaves go back to work. I heard a few grunts from their physical and mental distress. I looked down at my body. For whatever reason, I saw right through the skin. I could see tiny seeds in my chest, but they floated around like feeding maggots. Knots in my stomach, feeling like tiny snakes wrestling and maneuvering around my intestines. Somehow I knew that these things inside were meant to kill me. And they were designed to take over my soul... forever. I knew that I had a different suffering than the slaves, but my pain stemmed from the exact same cause.

I looked around me, and as I did, I noticed their singing growing a bit louder. It was a song I had heard my mamma sing.

"In the morning when I pray, in the morning when I sing, we'll go sweeping through the heavenly city..."

I began to sing along, at first with a little humming. But, afterwards, in perfect harmony. Suddenly, the sun began descending over the fields. The slaves continued to toil relentlessly... agonizing labor that bore no earthly reward...

Then, in my dream, I saw a man standing beside me who seemed almost disfigured from beatings. He slowly looked up at me. He had the same lowly motions and despair as George and Mamma did when they looked at me that way. Somehow I just knew… he had been cursed, just like them, but his curse was much worse. He lifted his rugged hands to take mine. I then saw these huge, bloody holes between his palms and wrists. He looked at me again. Tears streaming down His face, he displayed the most fascinating smile… a smile that contradicted His state of being… a smile that portrayed an unusual state of utmost Authority… and then He said, "This is not my kingdom…"

My eyes shot open as I woke up. Instantly, I had the answer I had been seeking. This was not His kingdom. If Henry was right, this was not their kingdom either. Which means this was not George's kingdom either. He, the man in the dream with the holes in his wrists, was doomed before George ever was. But persecuted? Why? The woman, the witch, with the magic powers? Her words popped into my mind causing me irritation that invoked a feeling of nausea before I even had time to bask in the interpretation of the dream. "One of you will go blind, and another will lose their mind…" George had given me that look before he went blind. And Mamma had given me that same look….

"Mamma!" I shouted, before realizing I was awake. That dream hopped me straight to my feet.

Everyone in my room was still asleep as I crept out the door.

There, still sitting in that rocking chair, was Mamma. Daddy was kneeling in front of her crying. She was wringing her hands, squeezing them back and forth, as he tried to pull them apart.

"Fee Fi Fo Fum, I smell the blood of an Englishman!" she railed. She laughed. She cried. She screamed. "Jesus, did you take my baby? I didn't take your baby! Fee Fi Fo Fum…"

"I can't get her to stop," he told me.

I had never seen Daddy look so helpless.

Later that day, more relatives came by to comfort Mamma and the rest of our family. I couldn't hear what they were saying to Mamma. But, before they had lifted her from the rocking chair, they asked us kids to go wait outside for a minute on the front porch.

I could hear her screaming inside the house as they tried to restrained her from going into a mental frenzy! I peeked into the window, as several men carried her into the bedroom. Daddy stood there, holding and shaking his head, not sure what to do.

The rest of the family whispered to one another as they left Mamma alone to rest on the bed... They began to argue.

"She's crazy..."

"She lost her mind."

"Shut up!"

"No, you shut up..."

Dead George was left lying there in the front room. Why didn't any authorities come to take George to the morgue or funeral home... or wherever...

The wolves prophesied to the sheep's destruction as the true shepherds fought...

We took Mamma to the psychologist for help, not a simple task. The white professionals took over and asked us to leave.

I then looked everywhere to find Daddy, but he was nowhere to be found. Unsure what to do, I listened to my siblings, in-laws, and others who had followed behind us to support Mamma and argue about Mamma's condition outside the office. They argued all the way back to the house. It was like watching a worthless parade. An ineffective parade, no adaptability, failing to adjust to the social construct of the march.

But who was to be blamed? What diagnosis was accurate?

I tried to gather my thoughts and wait, until I could stand no more. I quickly grabbed my bible, threw on a coat, and ran to the park.

Most of the trees by now had nearly lost all their leaves, but a few stubbornly held on...

I started to write a poem...

A pretty bushel of orange and yellow leaves still sit in the tree, from last year's conclusion, the ending of summer, spreads into the ending of spring. Finally dies out at the last of fall and drops into winter with a heavenly fall.

I was on a mission to go to the place in the bible where Henry had made me read the part that revealed that the Hebrews were the ones placed on ships, headed to bondage. I knew that it was the book of Deuteronomy...

"Hmmm", I whispered. "I think it was chapter twenty-eight..."

Finally, I found it. It was the very last verse in chapter 28... verse 68. There it was! I read it again, and all the verses that preceded it. But it was verse 65 that took me by surprise!

As I read it again, I could barely breathe!! My heart began pounding out of control. It felt like it would leap out of my chest. I couldn't believe it...

"And among these nations shalt thou find no ease..." I read out loud, hearing footsteps in the leaves.

I watched two young white boys walk by, the same ones I had threatened to hit after they called me a nigger. This time, they left me alone, but I heard them laughing as they spoke to one another, cautiously glancing my way.

But my mind was somewhere much more important now... I now thought about the plight of the tribe of Judah... the black Hebrews.

"And among *these* nations... shalt thou find no ease, neither shall the sole of thy foot have rest: but the Lord shall give thee there a trembling heart, and failing of eyes, and sorrow of mind."

How could this verse be so accurately describing my family at this precise hour?

At that exact moment, my heart could not stop trembling...

George's eyes had failed him... and Mamma seemed insane due to her sorrow of mind... God, right here, was talking about a People, *our People*, Henry had taught me.

"And our People were doomed," Henry's words echoed in my memory. "And they would be scattered among all other people, among their enemies, among the heathen. That's what's happening to us as the black Jews, as God's... He's chasing away his Children... And He's placed us among the godless."

Everything was starting to make sense now. But it only made sense if Henry's theories were correct.

All of our oppression, our history... Daddy's troubles... Mamma's curse... George's death... slavery... being called a nigger and isolated... the hatred aimed towards us for no reason...

Other than *the color of our skin, what was it?*

*O*r maybe the real reason was for something else?

What if the hatred wasn't because of the color of our skin? I wondered now. What if it was because... Because we are His People? Our identity itself? What if it was... *Us?*

The hatred would then be... more than we understood.

Spells, witches, lynchings...

I was always trying to figure the reasons. I thought... *Maybe our people are trying to connect dots in a realm where the dots are invisible...*

But what do I do now? George is dead. Mamma's been taken away. Daddy's out... who knows where, and all I hear from every other family member is fighting or blame...

"They are falling right into the trap the heathens wants us in!" I muttered, as I stood up. "Self-hatred... Hatred for our own People..."

"Henry," I said, trying to refocus.

I needed to know more. This was Saturday. I was so worried about Mamma. Home was the last place I wanted to be, but I had to do something to help Mamma.

I ran as fast as I could towards Henry.

'Oh gosh,' I thought! 'It was night, the skies were dark, and I failed to memorize Henry's exact location'.

As I reached the train tracks in the general vicinity, I saw several hobos. At a distance, I saw that they were all light-skinned with long, dirty hair, so I knew Henry was not among them. There were five in all, warming themselves by a fire. At least three of them had a bottle of something in their hands. I kicked the leaves as I approached, so as to not startle them too badly.

"Well, well... look at this pretty, young thing," I heard one of them blurt out.

"Have you guys seen Henry?" I asked, ignoring their glances.

"Who?" one of them mumbled.

"A black man around here named Henry. He has a dog named Trixie..."

"You know, Professor," another one said with a long, braided beard. "Professor."

"Oh, yeah, Professor," the first one said. "That arrogant darky. Yeah, he's about a half-mile yonder." He pointed further north up the tracks.

"Thanks," I said, rushing off.

"Why don't you stay here with us?" I heard in the distance, long after starting towards Henry's direction.

Trixie, again, sounded the first alarm, just as I arrived close to Henry's tent. Henry peeked out with his shirt unbuttoned.

"Well, hello there, young lady," he uttered with sincere delight. "Excuse me, while I get dressed."

I watched him politely enter his tent, wondering how a hobo could have so much courtesy. As he opened the tent, I could see stacks and stacks of books inside. He appeared back outside and fully dressed.

"What can I do for you, Betty?" he asked, as he moved past me to poke the logs ready to restart a fire. "You want to hear more 'bout who you are?"

"Not right now," I muttered. "They took my Mamma away."

"Who took her?"

"I don't know... Daddy, uhhh... well, we... took her to the doctor. She was talking out of her mind, and Daddy couldn't help calm her. She was crying really bad and making herself wild... and... and... screaming... a lot..."

"Well, her son just died, right?" Henry replied. "That's reasonable. She might be kind of... not in her right mind for now... well, at least not right away."

"It's more than that," I explained. "Not too long ago, this white lady all dressed in black told us something pretty bad. She came right up to our house. She told us that we were cursed. She said that one of us would go blind and another one would lose their mind... And she said our house was 'wished in death', whatever that means..."

"Oh, well, you can't believe all that mumbo-jumbo sorcery..."

"Yeah, Henry, but it happened. It's all coming true. My brother, George, he went blind right after that. And then Mamma…"

Henry went right back into his teaching. "We've been unfortunate here anyway," Henry interrupted. "With or without witchcraft, we've been taken away from our homeland. We've been brought low, but really we are the jewels of God. We're serving a country of people who are not our own. Now see, our citizenship belongs in heaven, and we are supposed to be separate from people that harm us. And now George is separate!"

Why did everything make so much sense when I spoke to Henry? Henry seemed to help me make sense of my dreams. Things that God had been saying to me came into view… with sudden clarity.

Yeah, that's why I ran back down here, I said to myself.

Suddenly, what we called "the gift" entered my mind… how we saw devils and angels… visions and dreams… Even accessing those things now made much more sense, but I didn't have time to deflect. I now had to know what to do about Mamma!

"Yeah, Henry," I shrieked. "I'm starting to understand it all now… But what do we do? And what about Mamma? What about the curses? What do we do now?… Are we all cursed without an option?"

Henry smiled. He seemed so happy that I had reached this point of reasoning so soon. He already knew that God had been dealing with me for a little while now. He even seemed to sense "the gift" and all that that entailed. Maybe he, too, had those spiritual insights. Maybe all black Hebrews have them…

"You tell me, Betty," Henry said. "What does someone have to do if they've been cursed?"

"They have to break it, I suppose."

"Very good, Betty," he said, matter-of-factly. "So break the curse."

"Please, Henry," I sighed. "I don't feel like teasing tonight, doing quizzes, or answering some kind of riddles..."

"Nothing is less of a game," he said sternly. His smile was gone. He frowned at me, and then his face eased closer towards mine. "Nothing is more factual. Nothing is more real. We are in a battle for our very souls! I'm not playin'!"

Henry's intensity, for a moment, seemed a bit scary. So I slowly moved away. His gentleman demeanor disappeared. Gripped by some ancestral force, the true Henry was gone. Unexpectedly, he had the look and spirit of a great warrior.

"Cursed is everyone that hangs on a tree," he hollered, quoting scripture while remembering how his own daddy died.

He explained that he was only a little boy when he saw it happen, but the memory seemed to cling to him like a branding iron etching a deep pattern within the shadows of his mind.

Dropping my head down in respect, I said, "I heard that in church... Jesus was hung on a tree, right?"

"Correct!" Henry responded angrily, making Trixie and me jump. "Yeshua was hung on a tree But why?"

"Because He was cursed?" I guessed. But I was lost.

"No, because He was afflicted for us."

"I don't understand," I sighed. I needed clear answers for Mamma... now!

"Okay, let's begin here," Henry said. He began pacing like he was teaching again in school.

As he began to explain again, I started to get confused once more. Henry noticed my puzzled look before proceeding. He stopped, walked a few paces, and looked down the tracks.

"Crucified thieves," Henry finally said. "We're all just crucified thieves, when you get right down to it..."

"What are you talking about now, Henry? I'm desperate to know!"

"So were they!" Henry snapped, as he whirled around walking in circles. "That's the point... Those people were far more hopeless than we, because they were on the brink of death!"

I knew that he had the answers I was seeking. So I relaxed now and decided to trust everything, every word he was going to preach. I composed myself with a deep breath. Henry had my full attention, and I listened.

"Two men were hung on each side of our Lord," Henry said, looking deeply into my eyes. "Two thieves... guilty and cursed. But Yeshua... although He was completely innocent, they condemned Him to die like us, alongside the guilty thieves..."

He stood up, looked into the woods, and squinted afar as if he could imagine the scene. A sudden breeze blew by.

"One thief found value in his evil life. He wanted to live, thrive, and carry on with his wretched ways. After taunting at Yeshua, he died. The other admitted his guilt and acknowledged Yeshua's innocence. He wanted to change and knew only Yeshua could do it. Inside, he knew that Yeshua was serving a death sentence that was not His. We're all cursed to die, but the second thief wanted a better life in eternity. So he asked for Yeshua's favor as he gave up his own guilt."

Henry knelt down in front of me. "And one day we will have a better life, too...."

"What did he ask for? Do you know?" I leaned forward with anticipation.

"To simply never forget Him. He knew that remembering Him when He went to His Kingdom would heal His suffering and His soul."

"To remember Him?" I felt a little disappointed.

"Of all the things to ask for in your last moments! The only One who could break the curse... I mean, why did He ask for *that*?"

"Don't you see, Betty?" Henry insisted. "That's everything..."

"No, I don't see..." I answered with frustration. "I would have told Jesus that I'm sorry... or something... for everything..."

My tears welled up, as I thought about the thief... as I thought about Mamma and my People in this world. Every emotion inside me was now gushing out, but I kept on...

"I'm hurting, and don't know what to do... That... that... that... I want to go somewhere else... I hate this world... I hate this world! I hate this world, Henry... They call us niggers... and... and... They called us darkies... And that... that... I... I'm...."

I dropped to my knees, sobbing. Hitting the ground with my right palm... I wanted to beat out every drop of torment and anguish that my family and I had gone through. What was happening? I wasn't sure, but I couldn't go on like this. There was no more pretense, no more barriers. I hated the world... I cried with sincere regret...

"I hate this world! I hate what people do... I hate that I hate..." Then the inner words came... "I hate myself!"

"Let it out," a Voice within me said. "A new birth is a new life. That's exactly how the second thief felt..."

Henry let me cry. He let me get every bit of it out without interrupting. He knew the importance of this moment. Finally, after he was sure that I was completely done, he stooped down beside me.

I felt like I couldn't move, so peaceful at that moment... I was almost scared to move. I didn't want this feeling to ever leave. I didn't want to go back to this world the same, this period in time.

"I want to give Him my life, Henry," I finally said. I wasn't completely sure where the words came from as they spewed out. But I was completely sure of their meaning, and I was completely sure they were mine. I owned them. I had to own them... It was my birth... This was the birth that I had control over...

For whatever reason, at that moment, I suddenly realized who Henry was. He was Henry Ridge, but they called him Professor... Of course! Professor Ridge!! My daddy's teacher! It was as if my eyes were now opened.

But I was enjoying this moment too much, and even Henry's sudden identity seemed of secondary importance to me. I breathed calmly now. I opened my eyes and saw my puddle of tears soaking into the cold ground. Though it was tears and not blood, it seemed as though I knelt on the scene of a battlefield. Like days of old, it seemed that great violence had occurred here. Breathing normally now, I was still frozen. My legs wouldn't move.

I could hear Henry still whispering... "In our dismal, short lives, that's all we really are... crucified thieves... Our position, our choice... our life... is just a slightly longer version of their abbreviated decision of an eternal destiny..."

"Remember me, Jesus," I whispered back. "When we're bein' divided... Remember me in your Kingdom."

Henry, loquacious as ever, spoke words so powerful, so intellectual, yet they easily penetrated my heart. A representation with no constraints.

I felt a silent Power... ... It seemed to come from the furthest galaxies... and yet reverberate back from the most infinitesimal particles. It transcended all civilizations from the beginning of time... and yet echoed into the realms of forever... The voice from the utmost Sovereignty... And yet it transfigured into a place of lowliness. From high, high above, the vibration traveled all the way down until it reached... me... Indescribable love... without limits, without boundaries... roared the sound of many waters... And yet, from a man, it was just a Whisper.

"You will be with Me in Paradise..."

11

"Warring Against Our Enemies"

Mamma was sent home, sometime while Henry and I had prayed. And partially due to the fact that our family had gathered outside again loudly demanding answers. She sat quietly in her chair with her head down and now seemed okay.

But now we had a new problem.

Daddy fought, asked, argued, and cried, but he had no luck with getting any true medical opinion about how George had died. For some reason, this small, humane gesture was needed by Daddy. I found out that Mamma had brought George to the hospital for tests after he had gotten kicked by the horse, and there was medical information on that. In addition, our primary physician had come to the house several times to check on George. The doctor was there after George had died to give an official "cause of death". He promised a copy would be available for Mamma within a day. The information was now on an official "certificate of death" at the hospital. But, for no other reason than to cause trouble during our time of grief, Sheriff Jimmy had gotten in the way and told the physician not to give it to us.

Who would stop a "certificate of death" to a grieving mother and father along with their family members? Only the devil, in my opinion... That same devil that had written "Timber fell on his head," for Uncle Joshua Euell Jackson... That same devil, who had delivered that false statement some years earlier, had returned to mock our family again. And now he was trying to deny a simple certificate that would provide my family with some sense of closure and just a small dose of dignity... the same certificate that white families received for every one of their deaths, without asking, without blinking, and definitely without provocation.

There was one difference here. Sheriff Jimmy didn't want us to feel like a normal family that suffered a tragedy... He wanted to do anything in his power, under his authority, to let us know that we... well, that we were... inferior and not worthy of the simplest of equal gestures... especially in death... especially when we were most vulnerable.

It's funny how, even today, the world will call anyone who protests against inequality names such as anarchists, terrorists, looters, and more. But keep going. They called us darkies...

Daddy had changed. Years ago, I don't think a "certificate of death" would have mattered to him. But now, with the way Mamma felt, and the fresh sting of George's death, Daddy seemed ready to go to war against all evil to access the smallest of rights, if not for himself, for Mamma and George.

Daddy was tired. He had reached a breaking point. Daddy wanted to explode.

I prayed for this one small victory, the Spirit of victory. I hoped that it would come to Daddy. He needed it.

Mamma had returned to relative normality in dealing with the mental stress of George's death. She quietly prepared for his funeral. The white church had "allowed" the service to be held there, most likely because George was my brother, and I had been attending dutifully for some time now. However, there would be a "church fee", and we would need a few volunteers to stay afterwards to clean up after the guests. And they told us that the preacher would take up a couple of collections, which would cover additional "funeral costs"… not just one collection, but two… one for the family, and the other for the church.

Daddy had spent all of his savings to get the casket and "a proper burial". He knew how Mamma felt about George. He was going to be sure to get the finest arrangements that he could afford, because, as I remember, many times the insurance company would charge the black families in town twice as much for burial insurance than most white families. So Daddy had saved in the case of another death.

As I walked in about thirty minutes early, I saw Daddy wearing his only suit, slouching in the front row.

There was no real family gathering. Daddy did what he could to arrange the date, time, and resources. The rest of the family continued to nitpick and squabble, as we each made our separate plans to "just get there on time".

I walked up to the open casket to see George. How differently he looked in death… so very peaceful. I knew that he wasn't there, but his visage reminded me of an old, favorite sweater I had owned. George loved that sweater, so I wore it at least twice a week, it seemed, even sometimes daily, wearing it through every kind of weather, until it grew too small. Afterwards, I hung it, ever so gently, on a hangar as it hung through space and time, year after year waiting... expecting George to return. No one understood the memories that it held for me. A lost beauty… of love, grace and happiness...

George looked as worn and out-of-place as that sweater. He just didn't fit in this world any longer.

I kissed George good-bye. His cold face....

I went and sat next to Daddy. I took his hand and held it, as I looked around at the church wondering which friends and relatives were attending the funeral session. Oh, there was Miss Ridge, my old teacher, sitting across the way. She smiled at me with the prettiest countenance, and I instantly smiled back.

I wasn't sure what Miss Ridge was doing now that the schools had been desegregated. As a matter of fact, I hadn't even thought about it much, and I felt a twinge of guilt. How wonderful of a teacher Miss Ridge had been to me and George. I glanced over again to look at her, but she had her neck swiveled towards something in the back of the church. She looked shocked, like she just saw a ghost. I looked back to see what Miss Ridge was doing, and that's when I saw him.

Professor Ridge stepped into the door. Grandeur, he was shaven and dressed to the nines! He had on a sharp, dark-blue suit, a silk red tie, expensive shoes, and a top hat.

Again, I had failed to make the connection that suddenly dawned on me. Professor Ridge and Miss Ridge! Had they been married? I was perplexed that I hadn't put that together, but, before I could do anything, I heard Daddy say, "Oh my God"! He, too, had spotted Henry, and walked back and embraced him in the aisle. They spoke quietly for a second, and then Henry followed Daddy to sit down with us.

"Betty," Daddy announced. "This is one of my oldest and best friends… Professor Ridge!"

But Daddy was shocked again when I shook his hand and said, "Thanks for coming, Henry…"

Daddy looked. "How do you two…"

Just then a white man tapped Daddy's arm, and Daddy turned to discuss some kind of business with him.

Henry sat down with me and took my arm. Sitting there silently, we both felt like we had mountains of support together. As Daddy continued to walk off and talk to various white men, I, again, thought about Miss Ridge and how she was connected to Henry. I looked over at her. She now seemed extremely uncomfortable! I had rarely seen the beautiful Miss Ridge in such distress before, and it took me a moment to connect the dots. I hadn't seen that look since... oh my God, since I had mentioned Professor Ridge to her that day in her classroom!

It took a large portion of the day to finally put George in the ground. Because blacks were not allowed in various parts of the cemeteries, Daddy had arranged for him to be buried as close to the most dignified, beautiful parts of the grounds as possible. To Daddy, George deserved this treatment, for he was the smartest man Daddy had ever known... far more intelligent, honest, and pure than the wealthiest of white men who were now dead, rotting corpses under magnificent headstones.

Henry stayed with us the whole day. Afterwards, he spoke with Daddy. And, before I knew it, they were walking to the sheriff's office.

"What's going on?" I asked them, catching my breath after following behind them. Henry now had a briefcase in his hand.

"We're going to try to get some business settled," Daddy said.

How exhilarating it was to see Daddy and Henry walking together on this mission. It seemed that Daddy had his confidence back. He had that look of self-assurance that I had been used to seeing. But, quite honestly, I hadn't seen that look on Daddy since... well, since that witch had visited our home, possibly setting all this tragedy into motion.

I suddenly had a bad feeling, as we approached the sheriff. I saw Billy, a snake of a man, that Mamma had warned me to stay away from. He eyeballed us as we approached, as he sat on a bench near the door, polishing his gun with a small, white towel. As we drew closer, he tapped the door loudly with his firearm to warn Jimmy, Cameron's longtime sheriff.

Jimmy came out of the door, his fingers went into his belt near his gun to intimidate us, who were now in front of the station porch. He stuck his chest out like a cowboy Napoleon.

"What can I do for you gentlemen?"

Billy gave a snort, while continuing to clean his gun.

Henry ignored their demeanor, produced some papers from his briefcase, and handed them to the sheriff. "We're here for the legal cause of death for George from your local hospital. We know that George's primary physician possesses one for the family."

"Last I heard, the hospital couldn't find those papers," Jimmy snarled. "Legal or not." He spit near Daddy's shoes. "And besides, it would take proper procedures or a court-ordered decision, for a medically described determination."

Suddenly, Jimmy moved next to Billy and spit some tobacco juice, this time near Henry's shoes.

For a minute or two, there was a standoff, as Jimmy, ignoring Daddy and Henry, read the paperwork that Henry had handed him.

"I think you got your answer, boys," Billy finally mumbled. "Now why don't you boys just..."

"Let me handle this, Billy," Jimmy jumped in. He had noticed something in the papers that bothered him. "Why don't you gentlemen come on inside my office?"

As Daddy went inside, Henry turned quickly to me. He spoke in a whisper so that Billy couldn't hear. "Betty, I want you to wait outside okay? Try to get a few witnesses to stand out here with you..." He winked. "... just in case."

I dutifully ran to my house and rounded up a few of my cousins, who were all in the house arguing with my siblings as usual. After several minutes of trying to convince them of our need for their help, they all decided to walk downtown and stand outside.

I ran ahead of them and peered into the window. Jimmy was as red as a tomato, yelling at someone on the telephone. Seconds later, he slammed it down. He pointed at Daddy and Henry, who were calmly seated in front of his desk. I could hear him yelling threats as he always did against black folks that questioned his authority. But he clearly hadn't gotten his way and was letting Daddy and Henry have a fresh earful.

Jimmy then signed a document before tossing it angrily towards Henry.

Henry placed the piece of paper into his briefcase. Then he stood up and quickly offered a handshake. Jimmy stood there, grimacing, refusing to respond. Henry quickly turned towards Daddy, tapped Daddy's shoulder, and headed for the door. Daddy stood, hesitated for another second or two, then followed Henry.

I don't know all that was said in that office, but Henry came out and announced to all of us, "Glad y'all could make it... Let's go!"

Without breaking stride, he headed towards the hospital and coroner's office. I looked back to see Billy and Jimmy standing, frowning, watching us walk away.

"I won't forget this!" Jimmy yelled.

"Keep walking," Henry said, ignoring Jimmy. He was already several yards down the street and walking briskly.

Daddy put his arm around me and grabbed my little sister's hand with the other. We marched behind Henry as the others followed, a mini parade of victory mixed with heartfelt fear.

This was as good as it got for hometown Negroes. I soared down the road, celebrating the "win" and ignoring the fear. Breaking into an impromptu skip, I felt like a child behind the Pied Piper. I knew we were going to get a real death certificate... a real answer! And these rare moments of celebration, no matter how small, were to be cherished.

During the mile walk to the hospital, I silently thanked the Lord. I had experienced only a small taste of what the slaves had felt just a hundred years prior.

How horrible not to be able to attain the most basic of rights in our human existence. We had it easy now. We were fighting for a death certificate. At one time, the slaves couldn't as much as fight to keep their families together. They couldn't even fight for their own lives.

How horrible to have a member of your family sold to be separated from the rest forever! The slaves had no say towards their preferences of where to live or who to work for. Their feelings were as countless as the animals'. Well... really, less than an animal. A husband had to watch his wife, as she was sold to a sadistic owner a hundred miles away, his eyes cast down to hide his horror, his shame... his love. Then he might be forced to watch his children, one by one, sold to others... his protective, natural, fatherly duties forsaken to avoid them, seeing his sure death if he stepped in.

The only hope of reunion was to live. The only hope was Life.

All of life's noble characteristics for mankind ... pride, love, independence, choice, self-sufficiency... were all dashed, or at least compromised for minorities, along with their very humanity, by the colonizers who ran the legal, political, and world systems.

We approached the hospital and proceeded to the part of the hospital that was only for blacks. It was an old, stone building with bars on the windows, just one step of taste above a common prison. I watched Henry as he walked more briskly, evidently trying to catch a man who was getting into his car.

"Mister Moore," Henry called out.

A white man with dark hair turned around, after placing his briefcase into his cream-colored Buick. He looked at Henry, and then nervously spotted all of us coming from behind him.

145

"Mister Moore, I have the proper paperwork signed by the sheriff to release the cause of death for George Jackson," Henry said. "Are you Administrator Moore?"

"Yes," he said, still glancing nervously towards us. "But there's no business after four o-clock."

"Sir," Henry said, with a professional demeanor. He looked at his watch. "It is only 3:37, and we got here as quickly as we could…"

"I'm sorry," he said. He quickly got into his car. He rolled down the window an inch. "Be here Monday at 9 a.m.," he shouted through the crack while slowly driving away.

"This is Thursday!" Daddy shouted back, not wanting to have this unresolved through the weekend. He also knew that this certificate, as tiny of a gesture as it was, might provide just a little encouragement, a little solace, a little humanity, for Mamma during this unbearable time. "We'll be here tomorrow!"

Mister Moore rolled down his window another inch. "I won't be here tomorrow," he said smugly. "I work only four days, Monday to Thursday…"

He spotted me next to Daddy and did that flirtatious looking... staring, looking up and down at my body parts, before giving me a quick wink. "Plus, I have a big golf tournament tomorrow!" he added before closing his window.

After hearing that, all we could do was watch him drive away, leaving us silently in the dust from the dirt road.

I could barely focus the next day at school. If anyone said 'nigger' or even looked at me wrong, I felt like I would explode. But to be honest, I wasn't sure if I would fight or look down and go the other way. I knew inside that releasing any anger would make matters exponentially worse for me, and my family didn't need more to deal with.

I couldn't stop thinking about George... and Mamma's pain. But Friday, the weekend, and Monday, came and went without incident. And, when I arrived home from school on Monday afternoon, there was Mamma in her rocking chair, smiling and calm in a pretty dress.

I was filled with joy... I ran and hugged Mamma with everything I had. What a different person she was after receiving clarification about George. Not real clarification, but I could tell she was happy to at least receive his death certificate. In it, the cause of death was described as fluids and pressure build-up inside of his brain, probably from when the horse had kicked him. What a long, slow death.

But this was the first halfway accurate death certificate that our family had ever gotten.

We felt somewhat like white folks, if only for a day. Amazing what a piece of paper can make one feel like...

Then I spotted Henry in the corner of the room. He was smiling in between puffs from a pipe he was smoking. I ran to him and hugged him also.

"Hey, do I get one of those, too?" Daddy asked. I hugged Daddy harder than the other two. "We're going to have a celebration tonight, Betty Bug. And you don't have to go to school tomorrow..."

"What?" I gasped.

"Hey, if Mr. Moore only works four days a week, my kids only got to work four days a week!"

That night, we celebrated. Family members from all over visited, joining the fun. George had just been buried, and it seemed everyone was looking for a reason to smile. The release of these simple papers easily fit the bill.

But, again as usual, the room filled the air with more bickering.

I had to get out. As I walked into the crisp, night air, I spotted Henry finishing his pipe and gazing at the stars. "It's cold out here, Henry," I said as I approached him. "You aren't going back down to the tracks tonight are you?"

"That's where I live," Henry said, continuing to look upward. "Besides Trixie needs me. She's probably waiting up for me like a worried wife…"

I thought about Henry for a moment, wondering why he lived outside. He still had on the same suit. As he started towards home, I yelled out, "Thank you, Henry! You are a good teacher, and you played a lawyer real good, too."

"I was a lawyer," Henry said over his shoulder. He stopped and faced me. "I was an attorney in Birmingham, and then a teacher there…"

"What happened?" I asked. "Why are you up here?" I walked towards him so he could speak quietly if he needed.

"My daughter is up here…" Henry said with a smile.

Suddenly I thought about Miss Ridge and her angry looks at Henry. "Is Miss Ridge your…"

"Daughter, yes," Henry said. "Although she hasn't spoken to me in some years…"

"Why?"

"We just had some misunderstandings…"

"Like what?"

Henry could see that I was intent on fulfilling my curiosity. He hesitated then went and sat on the edge of the nearby park bench so he could tell the story. I quickly sat on the ground in front of him, legs crossed, ready to listen.

"Long ago, it seems, my wife died from leukemia," Henry began. "I had switched from being a lawyer in Birmingham to

148

convincing my wife into moving to Wiley College in Texas. I had been offered a teaching job there. All the great black educators seemed to be gathering at Wiley to teach a generation of hungry, black youth with great futures... My lovely wife left all her friends, and we moved to Texas with our daughter, Andrea."

"Who?"

"Your Miss Ridge," he politely corrected.

"Sad, I guess you'd say, huh?" He gazed up at the stars again. "Evelyn, my beautiful wife, the one who always supported my selfish desires... She immediately got sick when we got to Texas, and..." He looked back at me with a sigh. "I guess I didn't handle her death very well. I didn't know the Lord; I didn't know nothing about being a Hebrew... and I just began to drink... a lot. I cared for Andrea... um, Miss Ridge... I worked at the College, and I would come home and drink like a sailor every night until I passed out... Eventually, I lost everything..."

"How?"

"I was in no condition to enhance the brightest young minds on the earth in my inebriated state..."

"What?"

Henry, lowering his head, said, "I wasn't able to do my job because I was an alcoholic... a self-pitying man in trouble. I couldn't hardly take care of myself. They fired me. By this time, Andrea had met a young man from Missouri, who promised to wed her later, if she acted like his mistress..."

"His what?"

"His wife..."

"Miss Ridge was married?"

"Not yet, and I wasn't going to allow her..." Henry suddenly kicked at the ground. He looked like he didn't want to talk any longer. "I wasn't a good person, and it takes one to know one, and... I strongly disagreed about her choice of a husband... He didn't love her, and he didn't treat her right... He was selfish, and I didn't like him... well, and..." He calmly looked back up at the sky.

"I regret that," he said softly. "Evelyn was gone, Andrea left for Missouri with her ... supposed fiancé... I had no job, and I used all my savings just to drink."

We sat silently for a while. I could hear members of my family screaming at each other in the far distance, so Henry and I continued to talk in the nearby park.

"So what happened next?" I asked, breaking the silence.

"Funny thing happened," Henry answered, changing his mood a bit. "Funny thing happens when you lose... everything. Because when you lose everything, you got nothing to lose..."

"What?"

Henry looked at me.

"My own mother had taught me about Yeshua before she died. And she told me, 'Henry, one day you'll have nothing, and you will need Him'.... And I guess I remembered her words. Her words became very clear to me after I lost all my material things..."

"Couldn't you become a lawyer or a professor again?"

"Funny thing," he said, "When the Spirit comes in, man's knowledge begins to seem really... stupid, for lack of a better word. Everything he does, to gain money, prestige, the 'American dream'.... It all really seemed backwards and ignorant. Representing the law seemed like slavery in a snake pit all of a sudden... And education, at least American education about black history, became the antithesis of truth!"

"The what?"

Henry smiled. "I didn't want to be a teacher or professor or lawyer any longer. None of these things seemed like they held any form of real truth... I quit drinking and I began to learn about my roots. I was only interested in one thing for about three years... studying the bible. I learned that I was a black Hebrew from the tribe of Judah, and I could hear my God speaking to me like I'm speaking to you right now." Henry shivered as streams of fog formed from his breathing. "But eventually I became homeless, and I caught a train up here to Cameron, where I heard... Miss Ridge was..." He looked down again. "I can hear Him. My only mission now is to do what God wants me to, and make it right with my daughter..."

"Why..." I wanted to phrase my question with empathy. "Why does she seem so..."

"Furious?" Henry finished. He tried to smile, but it turned sour when he said, "Hell hath no fury like the scorn of a woman..." He took another deep breath. "In a nutshell, I found her up here living in... well, the man never intended on marrying her, I don't believe. I got mad at him over and over... I told her that I was... different now. That I was sorry that I hadn't been there for her when her mom passed. Then I tried to run away the man who she mistakenly thought was there for her. The man left her, like I supposed he would, but she had her education by then. She got a teaching job and lived by herself, and she told me to stay away. I guess she felt like I was responsible for losing... what little she had... I guess I wasn't there for her... when she needed me to be... She went from two parents to no parents, because of my self... indulgence and..."

"She didn't let you live with her?"

"We disagreed on her man," Henry explained. "But I think she also blamed me for her mom's death. We were always fighting about that move to Texas. Andrea and I disagreed on almost everything... She was into education, the American dream, ambitious. She was doing all the things young kids should do... And I guess I had just learned what a deceptive facade all this had become..." He glanced towards two squirrels busily collecting acorns for the winter before speaking on. "And then all my drinking... I really hurt her a lot... said a lot of things, did a lot of things... I'm not proud of."

I understood enough. I wanted to change the subject.

"So why did you come today and do the work of a lawyer?"

"It was the only way to get your Mamma those papers she needed," he said softly. "Plus... I do what my heart tells me to do. I love your family, and God gave me the means to keep them together. It would be wrong of me to look the other way. That doesn't mean I'm going to practice law again..."

"Why not?"

"For one thing, they took away my license," Henry said with a smile. "But don't tell Jimmy and Billy that, for God's sake." His eyes followed a police car that passed by. He took a deep breath.

"I came not to bring peace," I said slowly, quoting Matthew. "I came to bring a sword." I'm not sure where the words came from. "... division."

Henry looked delighted all of a sudden. "And a man's foes shall be..."

"... they of his own household," we finished the verse together.

"The Lord speaks to you, Betty," Henry said. "You have a Gift. Don't ever take that for granted!"

That evening Henry returned to his "home" near the tracks... And that evening I learned that everyone has obstacles... an evening and a teaching not far removed from my 'new birth'... It was then that I realized that I was to use my Gift like Henry was using his. I was empowered with a Spirit, and it wasn't just to control evil or win arguments... It was to promote truth and guide men to freedom!

But confrontations were bound to happen… And I fully admit that I sought out the clash that followed at the white church. For some reason, I just had to do this. It was my own initiation. This would be my first test, my opportunity to confront a church that had taught me false doctrines and had charged my Daddy far too much money just to say a few words before his son was buried. All of this sat in my stomach like TNT just waiting for a spark…

It happened as Glenda, the pastor's wife, was decorating the church for Christmas day. It was Friday afternoon now and the last day of school before Christmas break. Soon the 1959 new year would be a reality…

"Hi," I said cheerfully. "Would you like any help?" But I felt like an assassin dressed as an innocent schoolgirl.

"Sure," Glenda said. "Can you get that ladder and hang these angels above the windows?" She handed me a pile of white angels.

"And then you could dust off the manger set that we just got out… I think it's pretty dirty…"

I hung the angels with some tape and glanced around the church as I usually did. Everything, everyone that was presented in the decorations and images were all white. I got down from the ladder and initiated a conscious effort to find the "half-face" of the black man in the very corner of the stained-glass window. There he was! Even the donkeys and sheep were in full view. But the half-face seemed smaller than ever now, a half-smile, and one eye, and the half-body barely protruding from the edge.

I picked up the baby Jesus from the large Nativity scene and prepared to dust him. I examined it before speaking.

"Did you know… that Jesus… was…" I looked up to make sure Glenda was listening. She glanced down at me while hanging the lights. "… not white."

I finished and held my breath. '*Here we go,*' I thought. But Glenda didn't seem to hear me.

I shuffled my feet nervously, glancing down at the false image of Christ. Trying not to break it, I repeated, "Not white, Glenda!"

Then a streak of boldness hit me like lightning. I set the Jesus down and lifted my head to speak directly to her. All that Henry taught me spewed out.

"I learned that Israel was filled with people of all shades of brown, because Israel was actually part of Africa. And, when the Romans rose up to capture or kill them, they fled to the mountains, like Jesus told them to. And they migrated into Egypt, the Sahara regions, and finally into the West Coast of Africa. And... and... um... Deuteronomy... um, I think it's..." I closed my eyes and tried my best to remember. "Deuteronomy, twenty-eight, sixty-eight... says that they will go into bondage with ships!"

I opened my eyes and saw Glenda staring down at me. She carefully and slowly came down off the ladder and sat on a pew. "Betty," she began. "You have been through so much. And I am so sorry about your brother..."

She patted the wooden pew to gesture for me to come over and sit next to her. I walked over and sat beside her.

"... And, Betty," she continued. "I'm so happy that we were able to be there to help your father with the arrangements and service..."

"Why did you charge my daddy that money?" I asked sharply. "You know my daddy didn't have no money, especially after paying for the casket, the burial, and everything..."

"Well, Betty... churches cannot do everything for free..."

"You're putting up those decorations for free. You bought that new organ... You helped Mister James buy a new car for Christmas last week." I stood and looked around. "You bought new carpet, new pews, and even put in a basketball gym next door that you never let my family play in..."

"But that's my point, Betty." She grabbed my hand. "These things are for our members, and they all cost money... And old things have to be replaced with new things..."

"Don't you think my daddy has to do that, too?" I asked. I hadn't realized how passionate I had felt to protect daddy. It was unfair to charge him that much money, and my 'color of Jesus' argument got pushed to the side. "There was nothing wrong with your old pews, your old carpet, and nobody plays basketball in your gym..." I began to feel tears coming, but I quickly brushed them back with a swipe from my fingers. "My daddy doesn't have money to replace his wooden floors with dirt holes in them or... or his rickety chairs... his money goes to put just enough food on our table for the day..."

I looked at Glenda with fire in my eyes. Angry for what the church did and passionate for truth, I continued... "And you made him pay... not to bury his son, but only to use your place for a few minutes and say a few words... so... so you could hang Christmas decorations? Why don't you do like Jesus did and help the poor?"

Glenda refrained from showing emotion. She stood and put her arm around me. "Oh, Betty," she went on. "In the bible the people just lay their tithes and offerings at the apostles' feet to use for the sake of the church."

"No," they entrusted the money at the apostles' feet so that it could be distributed to support everyone in the church, especially the poor... Remember that 'orphans and widows' part?"

Glenda went to the altar, knelt down, composed herself, and placed her hands as if to pray. "Do you want your daddy's money back, Betty? Is that why you're here?" she asked, looking up at the cross.

"No... I said calmly. "No... I didn't plan on saying none of this. I... I just came to tell you that you were wrong about what you taught me a while back... You know, about one of the wise men being black, although he might have been..."

This was not going at all as I had planned. I took another deep breath. "Glenda," I began again. "I've been studying and... learning. And... well, almost every important person in the bible was a person of color..."

Glenda looked at me with a blank look... waiting...

"Black," I added. "And He loved everyone and treated everyone with fairness."

"Oh, Betty," she said "You haven't joined one of those radical groups from Kansas City have you? Where are you getting this nonsense?"

"From the bible," I said clearly. "Did you know that they confused Moses, Paul, and Joseph with Egyptians? And we know that Egyptians are brown and black... And... and John the Revelator said that His feet looked like burnt brass, and the Person on the throne looked like jasper and sardine. Mr. Henry taught me that. Those are all dark colors, and... and all this is in the bible. You know, the bible that y'all read."

She sat there very still, nodded at me and waited again...

"And the people that were called Israel left Israel," I went on. "Well, I mean, you know that much from Joseph and his brothers moving to Egypt. And... and... and the bible said that his People, Israel, would be scattered throughout the nations."

I was now getting excited as my teaching from Mr. Ridge came flooding back. I was hoping that Glenda would see me differently as I explained these things that she didn't know.

"And, like I said, we were always in bondage, caught up in religions that charge money for the poor to bury their dead, and who tolerate slavery, for example. And we went into slavery again with ships... That's the Transatlantic Slave trade, Glenda!"

Glenda looked pale.

"Are you okay Glenda?"

She stood and walked away from me slowly, placing her hands over her heart, before turning back towards me. She sighed then calmly said, "First of all, Betty... My name is not Glenda to you. My name is Sister Blackburn, and I am the pastor's wife. Please show some respect."

She walked a few paces away then slowly wheeled around again.

"Secondly... just take a look around, Betty! These beautiful paintings, stained-glass windows, the wonderful Jesus hanging on the cross..."

She moved towards the Nativity scene. She put one hand on Joseph's head, the other on Mary's. "All of these images are white people for a reason. These are years and years of research from scholars and priests... and men of God. Around the world, Jesus and his people... Betty, you know they don't look like you."

"They're wrong," I said bluntly. "And, besides that, Yeshua speaks to our family. At least that's what Henry called him. We have a gift. I've heard God and... and seen angels... and..."

"That's enough, Betty," Glenda snapped. "The Spirit of God doesn't speak to people like you..."

She took a deep breath and managed a smile. She lifted her palms in each direction, as if to motion for me to look around at the surroundings. "God speaks to teachers and preachers... like my husband and I... people who have dedicated their lives to His cause..."

"You mean, white people," I blurted out.

"I mean teachers and preachers, like my husband and I."

"God has spoken to me more times than I can count! He speaks to all of my family. He speaks to Daddy all the time. He speaks to all of us... And... and... I have dreams and visions, like the bible says. I've seen angels... They came and took my grandmother to heaven... I've also seen devils, even right in this church... And... and I learned... from the bible... from Henry... that we black folks are God's people, too..."

"Betty!" Glenda shouted. She was now growing irate. "And you think that centuries of scholars and great American ministers are wrong, and... and a little colored girl from little 'ol Cameron... whose... whose darky daddy is a trash man... knows more than they do? Don't be silly, Betty..."

She sat restlessly as if trying to think of what to say. She tried to compose herself.

"Glenda..." the pastor interrupted. We hadn't seen him peek in through the doorway that led to his office. "What's going on?"

No answer.

"What's going on here, Betty?" he asked, without looking at me.

No answer.

"Just take it easy, darling," the pastor said softly. "Just calm yourself, Glenda..."

He looked seriously concerned.

"I was just tellin' her, sir... " I began. "That God's chosen People are..."

Then Glenda erupted into a wild rage finishing my sentence.

"... are niggers!"

"Glenda", the pastor politely said. "We don't use that word in here!"

"Why not?" Glenda replied, glancing up walking toward her husband. "You use it at home all the time... And... and it's just..." She looked at me, stuttering before finishing. "... Betty!"

I was so shocked I didn't know what to say. I stared at the pastor, hoping he would help me.

"She questioned our fees," Glenda screamed. "She questioned our beliefs. And I'm pretty sure she is thrilled to have upset me!"

The pastor went over to his wife and held her hand to calm her.

"Let us now pray," the pastor whispered while closing his eyes.

I felt a twinge of embarrassment.

12
"Henry's Departure"

After leaving the church, I went into the house where groups of people were visiting. Some of the people I didn't know. No one paid me any mind at all. Feeling invisible, I went into my bedroom and looked out the window facing the street. I could see Daddy and Henry in a heated argument of some sort. I wanted to know what they were talking about, so I slowly lifted the window just a couple of inches. The noise in the house was too loud. I placed my ear next to the opening.

"But this is my home, Henry," was all I could hear, as Henry and Daddy continued their conversation.

After a few minutes, I saw Miss Ridge pull up in front of the house. I saw clothes and even some small furniture that filled up her back seat. She jumped out smiling, and I saw her walk quickly over to shake hands with Daddy.

I couldn't wait any longer. I had to know what was happening. I ran out of my room, past all the arguments, and out the door.

"What's going on?" I shouted.

Henry turned and addressed me. "Betty, we are leaving."

"Okay," I said. "So I'll see you tomorrow?"

"No, Betty," Henry said, slowly lowering his head. "We are going back South... for good. I could get my daughter a teaching job by next week..."

"The South sounds wonderful," I exclaimed. I felt like crying. I felt desperate. "Can I go with you?"

Daddy looked surprised.

Henry glanced over at him, nodded his head, and walked over to me. He put both hands on my shoulders. "Betty, the South is not wonderful," he said softly. "No place around here is really... wonderful." Henry stopped and smiled slightly.

I turned and spotted Miss Ridge. She was smiling, too! One of the prettiest smiles that I had ever seen. She seemed to have a glowing countenance that indicated she had been meeting with her dad, and they had patched things up. While I was facing a few of my own demons, it seemed they had both overcome many of theirs.

I was going to miss them. I felt slightly guilty that my selfish feelings overshadowed their victory. I wanted to cry.

Henry saw that look in me, as he always did. He began to speak to me again. "You remember I told you that I came up here to rescue my daughter?"

"Yes, Henry."

"Well, my mission is accomplished," he said. "We need to leave. I need to take her away from here. It's too dangerous now. And, besides, we... she... we... just don't belong here anymore."

I heard a glass shatter and noises of laughter coming from the house.

"Sometimes I don't think I belong here either, Henry," I said sadly.

"None of us really belong here," Henry said. "God speaks to you, so you know what I mean... None of us *really* belong." He lifted my chin and looked into my eyes to make sure I understood. "But this is where you need to be right now... With your family. And I need to be with mine."

I hugged Henry as hard as I could.

"You'll always be my family," I said. I tried to lighten my mood as I mimicked him. "God speaks to you, so you know what I mean..." I stopped and smiled. "You'll always be my family..."

Henry hugged me back. "One day all this will be over," he whispered. "You know what I mean, too."

With that, Henry turned and walked towards his daughter. She gave a quick wave and her beautiful smile once more.

They got into the car.

Daddy put his arm around me, as we watched Henry give one last wave. The car started slowly down the dark road towards the South.

Oh, how my heart ached.

Though I was happy for Henry and Miss Ridge, I knew that I would never see them again. I felt joy for Henry, sadness for me, and the sorrow of losing a friend, all at the same time. Oh, how I would have loved to go with them, to leave this oppressing state, to leave the friction of my home. I trusted that Henry was right, there was no place we really belong. I knew what he meant, that there was no place free of racism against our people. I needed to be here, just like Henry had needed to be close to Miss Ridge until the time was right.

I wasn't sure if I would end up being the rescuer or the rescued, either option seemed enchanting. But I needed to be here for my own family.

For some odd reason, even surrounded by family, I now felt lonely. Snowflakes began to fill the night air reminding me of that wonderful evening I had met Henry by the tracks.

I ran into the street and watched the tail-lights disappear...

Forever...

... Into the night.

13

"Living THEIR Dreams"

As time went by, I had graduated high school and was now working most days, all day, cleaning the homes of several white families.

Two years had elapsed since Henry and Miss Ridge's departure, when I received a phone call from Henry. Their absence had left a hole in my heart, and I had secretly wished they would return. But, deep inside, I knew it was best that they were forever gone from Missouri. I had prayed to see them again. And then one day...

"Betty, Betty, Betty!" he shouted playfully, after Daddy handed me the phone. I could actually feel his longing of missing me in his voice, a voice that I had forgotten, but missed like family.

"Hi, Henry," I replied. I wasn't sure why I suddenly felt depressed. "How are you and Miss Ridge getting along?" I tried my best to sound exhilarated.

"We're doing great," he answered. "Andrea already has a full-time teaching job. She is so happy. And Wiley College actually hired me back. I'm working again as a professor! You should come down here now, Betty. I could get you admitted into the college!"

Daddy, listening, paced slowly away. I watched his stride. He slightly limped from a difficult walk that he tried to hide. He now owned several trash trucks and had several young men working for him. But the years had taken a toll on Daddy... Although a part of me wanted to jump on the first train south, I instinctively felt I was needed in Cameron with my family.

"Maybe one day..." I said slowly. I wanted to go there so badly, but Something compelled me to stay. In my heart, for a reason unknown, I felt that my family was going to need me soon. I knew that Henry could hear the unhappiness in my voice. "Hey, Henry," I uttered, changing the aura. "How's Trixie doing? You took her, right? I bet she really likes the warmer weather in Texas..."

I hadn't seen Trixie since that joyful night by the campfire, and always wondered if Henry took her. 'Why wouldn't he?' I had asked myself. I had stopped thinking about her after their departure.

There was a long pause...

"Henry?"

"Um, Betty," he moaned. "I know you really loved Trixie, and so did I... I don't know how to make this sound pleasant, but I've always been truthful with you..."

"What, Henry... Just spit it out..."

"Trixie died," he answered. "Before we left Missouri... Somebody or somebodies killed her... I will spare you the details, but I know that it was a warning to me. That's partly why we left so quickly that night... I didn't want you to worry."

"What did they do to her, Henry?" I interrupted. I wanted to know.

"Betty, you don't want to know..."

"But I do, Henry! What did they do?"

"Let it go, Betty," he pleaded. "That was two years ago..."

"Tell me, Henry," I said sternly. "I'm not a girl anymore. I have to live here, Henry. I loved Trixie... You owe me at least that... I want..." I took another breath. "I need to know what happened."

"I don't know for sure what all they did to her," Henry finally said. I could hear the pain in his voice. "It happened that morning sometime... The morning before my daughter and I left."

"What happened, Henry?"

"I don't know, Betty," he said, buying time. "I woke up and Trixie was gone... I... I... I remember looking all over for her. She usually comes right away when I call her. I knew something was wrong..."

"What?"

"I was walking through those woods and I just walked up and... and I saw my dog hanging from a tree... Noose tied around her neck. Unfortunately, no, fortunately... I don't know what all they did to her, Betty. And... and there was a note nailed to her bloody, lifeless body..."

"A note?" I repeated, but it made perfect sense if they were warning Henry.

"What did it say?"

"I never... I... I never lied to you, Betty, "but... but you don't... need to be bothered with all this... You don't need to know all this mess. It was meant for me..."

But I kept pushing. I just had to know the whole sickening story, it seemed, for that chapter in my life to make total sense.

Henry took a long, deep, breath before giving in.

"It said, *'Nigger lives matter even less'*" he answered slowly. "... with a few misspellings..."

I instantly knew that it was Jimmy, Billy, or one of their KKK cronies. They were secretly after Henry ever since he had helped Daddy, posing as an attorney.

"I have to go, Henry," I finally said, after yet another long pause. "I'm real happy for you and Miss Ridge..."

"I'm sorry, Betty," he said.

He promised to stay in touch before hanging up. But, as often is the case, that was a courteous form of a hopeful good-bye. It would be years before I would hear from Henry again... one last time.

The seasons came and the seasons went, as I grew into a full woman of 25-years-old. Men would come by to "visit". They would ask me out, trying to pull me away from Daddy. The right one had never surfaced though, so I locked myself into the daily grind of working to bring in money by cleaning homes. I wanted to do all I could to help support the family.

My sister, Esther, though only seventeen, had married her sixteen-year-old boyfriend, James Glen. And together, along with their ten-month-old baby, James Anthony, Jr., they, too, were now living with us in the home. Everyone called the baby Tony.

The 1950's had been a wondrous and changing time in America. Our country was hungry to feast on their new theme and identity after World War II ended. People were making more money, and the fast-moving entertainment industry fit the "desire for diversion and fun" menu perfectly.

As a result, the television had made its way into many homes in the 1950's, making this new, exciting recreation accessible to small hometowns, towns like mine. Daddy didn't want anything "as senseless, as controlling, and as expensive as a box telling us what to watch, feel, and do with our time." But most people did, and I found myself flipping on the televisions that were in all of the white homes I cleaned.

Television was fascinating to me. It allowed me to see things I never knew were out there. I saw people climbing and hiking through indescribable mountain ranges, living and working in tall skyscrapers, bustling in crowded cities and streets, and balancing themselves on a board that rode on top of the ocean waves!

But, most of all, to me, television defined normality and success in our land. I quickly realized how unusual our home had been all along. There was no farming, hunting, and fishing on television... no senseless bickering, at least not yet. There were handsome men wearing fancy suits, exquisite women wearing silk and lace in the latest fashions, and even children who sang and danced with glorious smiles and strange accents. I even saw some black actors, but playing parts that seemed strange to me. They looked different, uncomfortable or something...

Television defined who was acceptable and successful in America. And most all of them were white. No wonder Daddy didn't want that "box" in our home. But I was addicted. I found myself dusting and cleaning extra quickly so I could sit down and watch my favorite shows.

Oh, how I enjoyed watching Clark Gable and Vivien Leigh in "Gone with the Wind". Gene Kelly and Debbie Reynolds seemed so happy in "Singing in the Rain". My eyes were glued to Marlon Brando's every move "On the Waterfront" and to John Wayne in "Searchers". I never laughed so hard as I listened to Abbott and Costello's comedy. I had never seen men as debonair as Gary Cooper, Rock Hudson, and the dangerous James Dean. More and more I despised the local men, black and white, whose brash, "backward" characteristics resembled nothing even close to these new "larger than life" heroes.

Oh, and the women... The persona of true beauty and true womanhood became alive in the likes of Betty Davis, Ginger Rogers, Jayne Mansfield, Natalie Wood, and Marilyn Monroe. These women were so different from Mamma... They wore amazing outfits, high-heeled shoes, and priceless jewelry. They flirted with men, smoked like men, and seduced men. And they made it so glamorous, so powerful... Now this surely was the definition of American beauty!

I found myself trying to imitate them and buy clothes that resembled theirs. I even tried to do hairstyles like theirs. I opened my bible less and less, and did my work faster and faster, as I looked forward to my daytime television shows. I forgot all about being a Hebrew.

Later in life, "The Ten Commandments", included Charlton Heston, Yul Brynner, and Anne Baxter. I knew better, yet I was enamored with the great biblical characters in the likeness of these Hollywood stars...

As the white folks stayed inside watching these amazing shows more and more, the few black folks in Northwest Missouri still maintained their customary ways of talking on the porches and telling stories. The black church became the meeting places for black families and very prominent places for those too poor or detached to be watching television.

We now had small black churches in Cameron, Plattsburg, and Saint Joseph, not to mention many in the Kansas City area. But we were only few in number, so I figured maybe we were unimportant. Our churches were different than those of the white folks. But we were happy in our churches with our God. I even dated a couple of the local, single preachers at the time, who seemed to be attracted to my "Hollywood" clothes and hairstyles. Amazing black women emerged on television. How inspired I was to see women of color working as sophisticated actresses.

But American ideas and entertainment were not limited to the television. The radio brought the radical changes of music into the home, and even Daddy had a radio, listening, while making repairs on his trucks.

Frank Sinatra, Dean Martin, Bing Crosby, and Tony Bennett sang their romantic songs. Johnny Cash belted out country hits that sounded somehow like life, love, and poetry.

With the swinging, twisting, be-bopping phenomena of this new music craze, something else happened. Black pioneers not only joined in, but they even bypassed and led the change of music that forever changed the American landscape. Amazing performers rose up like Chuck Berry, Bo Diddley, Fats Domino, Little Richard, Ray Charles, and Nat "King" Cole. And white America, not only listened to them, they bought into their remarkable trends of musical expression that had been, undoubtedly, influenced and incorporated from past histories ranging from spirited African drums to long bouts of slavery oppression. The natural, black talent of music paved, seemingly, the first road to American black pride, equality, and acceptance.

Political agendas, racial hatred, and economic inequalities were no challenges in limiting black music, whose talented pioneers needed no such advantages. The "Juke Joints", "Blue Rooms" and "Jazz Clubs" sprouted like wildflowers even in the poorest of black neighborhoods.

For every "Luck Be A Lady" from Frank Sinatra, there was an equal or better "Mona Lisa", "Too Young", "When I Fall In Love", or "Smile" from Nat "King" Cole. For every "Hound Dog" or "Heartbreak Hotel" by Elvis, there was a "Tutti-Frutti" or a "Good Golly, Miss Molly" by Little Richard. For every "Great Balls of Fire" by Jerry Lee Lewis, there was a "Johnny B. Goode", "Rock N' Roll Music", or "Maybelline" by Chuck Berry. And for every "That's Amore" by Dean Martin, there was a "Blueberry Hill" or "Ain't That a Shame" by Fats Domino.

These black musical pioneers had the same agenda as the white ones, to sing of life or to tell a story. And most of America saw the commonalities of black people with their own. "Why, just listen to the words of their music..." they would rave. We weren't a strange people, after all! We had the same feelings as everyone else who came to America...

Looking back, I don't know if that was a good thing or not...

But, for better or for worse, black pioneers forged ahead by creating an even more unique expression of their inner selves in the form of jazz and blues. The local Kansas City jazz clubs were only a few years removed from their potent New Orleans roots. White men and women could only watch, enjoy, and try to copy, if they dared, the natural proficiency, smooth skills, and genuine, deep, dark expression of bebop, hard bop, cool jazz and blues through musicians such as Charlie Parker, Dizzy Gillespie, Miles Davis, John Coltrane, Thelonious Monk, and many others. I was fixated by the alluring enticement of the amazing women who came into prominence right along with these wonderful, new sounds: Sarah Vaughan, Dinah Washington, Nina Simone, and the effortless croons of Billie Holiday.

One night, a male friend of mine took me to the 18th and Vine area of Kansas City. We passed into a dark club, winding around dark, exciting people of my proud race. I felt so alive, so invigorated, so mysterious! He was able to get us seats at a smoke-filled, not-far-removed-from-the-stage table. As I began to sip my drink, a loud, penetrating bass sound echoed from a small stage. The reverberations seemed to grasp my soul and then my heart. Soon the lonely horns demanded top attention, pausing only for the smooth melody of the slinky saxophone. The rhythmic, joyous keyboard came right in. The loud sounds were so full of pain, joy, love, and hatred all at the same time. They were unmatched, until an unexplainable, indescribable voice bellowed out... from the "First Lady of Song" and "Queen of Jazz", Ella Fitzgerald. I had never seen or heard anything even remotely close to what I was seeing and hearing.

And it changed my life. From that day on, I was singing. Although my voice was far lower and, of course, nothing like Ella, many people seemed to love my baritone adaptations of many songs.

Later in life, I would sing at many churches all over Northwest Missouri.

But, for now, there seemed no end to what talented, creative Americans of the black culture could achieve in music. Duke Ellington took his big band and swing sound all across the globe, playing more than 20,000 high energy performances in front of wide-eyed, white audiences. Venues such as the Apollo and the Cotton Club, both in Harlem, New York, paved the way for the later, huge success of Berry Gordy's Motown Records in Detroit.

Through music, television featured the portrayals of a fish-eyed, balloon-cheeked Louis Armstrong or a funky, boogie-woogie, crazy-legged Chuck Berry as black representatives. For blacks and whites, music seemed to erase the past portrayals of black men, which had ranged from "angry and dangerous" to "scared and apologetic". These men were now bold, polished ground-breakers to America's love affair of "music that made you move". They were not just "run-of-the-mill" participants, they were the most radical leaders of the most radical craze.

Music soon gave way to other art forms such as writing. Gwendolyn Brooks received the Pulitzer Prize in poetry in 1950. Also, in the early 1950's, Ralph Ellison published "Invisible Man", quickly followed by James Baldwin's "Go Tell It On the Mountain". These masterpieces allowed all of the world to peek inside the oppressive conundrum of the racist reality for blacks inside of a white world.

Another area of influence that the black race achieved in America, and greatly enhanced in the 1950's, was in the form of athletics. Sports fit the temperament, coordination, and natural abilities of blacks like the fateful shoe fit Cinderella's unassuming foot... suddenly changing her direction and destiny to unknown heights.

There had always been isolated individuals, such as Jack Johnson, who, in 1910, had won the heavyweight boxing title over a man who claimed he "would prove that the white man is better than the Negro". Johnson walloped this forgotten man named Jeffries by knocking him out while causing ensuing riots all over the country. This boxing victory led to black eminence in the sport, starting with Joe Louis, who held the heavyweight title from 1937 to 1949, an astounding 140 months. This was the longest streak that a heavyweight title had been held.

I still remember Daddy hunched over his primitive radio listening to a Joe Louis match. Whether you recall Muhammad Ali, Sonny Liston, Sugar Ray Robinson, or Sugar Ray Leonard, the boxing titles and all its world rankings boasted of mostly black conquerors. And they still do…

Yet still, among most sports venues, blacks were banned to participate. And, when they finally were allowed, they had to, not only accomplish their craft physically, they had to also prove to be superior while enduring the mental, emotional, and psychological abuse of the stinging racial slurs from bigoted fans in the audience.

Just like music, when the door finally opened for many black athletes in the 1950's, they responded with complete success. In many ways, they dominated.

We always loved baseball in Missouri, and, in the '50's, we had the Negro Baseball League to enjoy in the form of our local Kansas City Monarchs, featuring future major leaguers like Ernie Banks, Jackie Robinson, Elston Howard, and Bullet Rogan. How boring the white, major-league games seemed on television compared to the talent and the antics displayed in the black games. America was able to finally enjoy a taste of that excitement when Jackie Robinson officially filled the void in 1947. But, before that, we were perfectly happy to witness, first-hand, the likes of Satchel Paige and Josh Gibson. Satchel was a 6'3" pitcher/performer, who could clown much like the Harlem Globetrotters with his high-leg kick and smooth delivery from all angles. In clutch situations, he would tell his three outfielders to sit down in the grass behind him! When they complied, Satchel could usually strike out the irate hitter with pitches that could "sink, wiggle, and even slither", according to Satchel. The Negro Leagues played with an intensity, an athletic ability, and with a level of comedy and theatrics that made the game much more enjoyable and exciting.

Jim Brown was the trailblazer in football, before hundreds, even thousands of black running backs, wide receivers, and others in every position would make up the majority of those on NFL rosters. Althea Gibson and Arthur Ashe opened the door in tennis long before the Williams sisters. And Charlie Sifford was able to break down the barriers in golf long before Tiger Woods. Amazingly, even basketball had been considered a white, "thinking man's" game until the all-black starting line-up of Texas Western stunned the all-white Kentucky team in the NCAA championship. Now look at the NBA players! I'm not even surprised anymore, as I still witness the rise of blacks in typical white sports such as wrestling, hockey, ice skating, speed skating, soccer, and so on…

The 1950's seemed to be the era when blacks began to rise, reign, and create a permanent dominion of creativity, inventiveness, intelligence, and talent. Black communities had their own businesses popping up like never before. Earlier in the century, a man named George Washington Carver, born right down in Diamond Grove, Missouri, had contributed immensely in the fields of botany and invention. Great mathematical assistance came in the form of black women for NASA to be able to send men into space and win their "race to the moon" over the Russians. Ralph Bunche won the Nobel Peace Prize for his ability to mediate the Arab-Israeli conflict in the Middle East. Johnson publishing company printed its first issue of

"*Jet*" in 1951. There was literally nothing that we couldn't do as a People, and I watched in awe as it exploded around me.

There were times that I would reflect on Henry's teaching and bask in the revelation that we are the tribe of Judah. The progress of blacks in every arena, but especially in music and sports, seemed to confirm that reality. Why it only made sense, I would reason, because God's People were worshippers and warriors. They praised and they battled throughout much of the old testament. So my logical theory was that these trends of success only duplicated the trend of our ancestors... We could and would ascend in these two areas that reflected our past giftedness and necessity we knew to follow our God. Even in slavery, we embodied song mixed with a physical prowess that contributed to our unmatched durability in Babylon, Assyria, Egypt, and, eventually, in the American fields of the South.

Henry's teachings, though, did not seem popular. Nor did his teaching seem to spread and become common. More and more, though, I saw their evidence all around me, the potency of that reality, that me and my blacks ancestors were brought here to America on ships, were taken from our land, stripped of our dignity, of our royalty and identity, and lost to foreign lands until Christ comes.

But, for me, this exhilarating truth that I learned from Henry began to slowly disappear like a fading dream. Forgotten...

The greatest moments for me of the 1950's, by far, were of the Civil Rights Movement that literally shook the world in the never-ending pursuit for equality. Oh, how the American clashes began when the Jim Crow segregation laws were resisted! It seemed that America is so nice when one cooperates with his evil agenda, but, oh, how he squirms, spews, and lashes out when one doesn't.

When the black soldiers victoriously arrived home after World War II, the German prisoners were fed and lodged on their way to be held in proper places... Our black servicemen? They were actually denied food and lodging in the South as they took their first steps back on American soil... still. These men, who were willing to die and who fought for our country, were repaid by that same country with unchanging, cruel hostility. These were the stories that Daddy told me.

It is an accurate depiction of one's true identity when they treat their enemies with higher love and dignity than their own defensemen. It is also an accurate depiction of identity when one is hated, though he did nothing but love. The Bible said, "Greater love hath no man than this... that a man would give up his life for his friends". We were friends, but not befriended.

For a black girl to get into a Topeka, Kansas public white school in 1951, it took the NAACP, a lawsuit, a denial by the U.S. District Court, an appeal to the U.S. Supreme Court, and three longs years before a unanimous decision on May 17, 1954 finally stated that the segregation of public school systems was unconstitutional. An NAACP chief council by the name of Thurgood Marshall, who would later become the first black member of the U.S. Supreme Court, advocated for that decision. This decision was called Brown versus the Board of Education. It took many states much, much longer to adhere to that ruling.

Change is a slow process. Righteousness comes even slower...

Besides Thurgood Marshall, many other men and women were willing to answer the call for change. Some paid jail and prison time for their answer. Some paid with their lives.

One of the latter group was a man named Malcolm Little, better known as Malcolm X. His teachings were beyond shocking at that time; that black people are the original people of the world, and that white people were not. He then prophesied the total destruction of all those that hate among the white race and among his own brethren.

How hypocritical that most of white America, back then, responded by calling him a hatemonger, a racist, and a black supremacist after hundreds of years of their people hanging the Negro. Blatantly stating that black people are not even human, promoting that whites are far superior, and, overall, attempting to annihilate or enslave our entire race, Malcolm responded back with a New York City national television broadcast about the Nation of Islam titled *"The Hate That Hate Produced"*. Ironically, though he would forever be known for his great fight and dialogue for civil rights, he rejected the civil rights movement and called for a complete separation of blacks from whites.

Two 1955 occurrences happened that thrust another man into that latter group of martyrs for equality. The first was tragic... A black 14-year-old boy named Emmett Till was brutally murdered while visiting Alabama, accused of whistling at a white woman. His mutilated, bloated body and face, in an open-coffin photo, was featured in *"Jet"* magazine and *"The Chicago Defender"* for all the world to see. This was the catalyst for the second occurrence instigated by a black woman by the name of Rosa Parks, whose refusal to give up her seat on a bus to a white person, invoked the year-long Montgomery Bus Boycott. A front and center spotlight was given to a young Christian preacher from Georgia named Martin Luther King, Jr., who organized the boycott and became the main leader of the world-changing civil rights movement. Mr. King, who believed in nonviolent protest, led marches for voting rights, desegregation, labor rights, and many other causes for lawful equality.

The 1950's produced quite a public stage as the Southern Christian Leadership Conference was ultimately founded, many blacks joined the cause, and daily speeches and columns calling for equality were "shouted from the mountaintops"! What an exciting decade to be a part of. Of course, many whites opposed the changes from Jim Crow laws, but, strangely, Mr. King also faced opposition from more militant blacks. Stokely Carmichael disagreed that integration would work, and Malcolm X called Mr. King a "chump" and other civil rights leaders "stooges" of the white establishment.

I decided to ask Daddy one day what he thought. He was working on one of his trucks, and I had just gotten home from cleaning three homes. "Integration or segregation?" I threw out at him..

"What're you carrying on about, Betty?" he asked, while still looking down at the engine.

"The Civil Rights arguments," I responded. "Martin Luther King is fighting for integration, and Malcolm X and other men think that is crazy. Will segregation work better?"

"If you're askin' if black folks can run themselves..." Daddy's head came out from under the hood. He looked at me with a small smile, as he wiped engine grease from off his hands. "They been doin' it for thousands of years in many parts of the world, and they been doin' fine... doin' it much better than white folks, if you ask me... 'Sides that, black people ruled the earth back in Egyptian times... most powerful nation in the world. But remember, they only became that powerful 'cause wise, little Joseph obeyed God's dreams. God made a whole nation powerful 'cause of one believer's dreams... along with his guts to stand behind them."

"And Joseph was black... right?"

"Sure, Betty, you know that. Joseph was from Israel. So, yeah, back to your question... segregation works good."

"Then why are we living with all these white folks?"

"'Cause this is our home," Daddy Joshua said. "And integration works better. And I'm doin' what God said, based on His dreams to me..."

He seemed done talking, turned, and put his head back under the hood.

But I wasn't finished. "Why do you say integration works better?"

"'Cause we s'posed to be doin' here on earth as it is in heaven," his muffled voice answered.

"Is heaven integrated?" I pressed.

"Yes and no," Daddy answered. He poked his head out again and looked over at me. "No, heaven ain't got no people who act with hate, so it's segregated. But, yes, heaven got all colors of People, so it's integrated. Doctor King just workin' based on his vision of heaven. This... this integration stuff... got to work 'fore we can get to heaven." He began to wipe his hands again while frowning. "Jimmy, Billy, and some of them Cameron church people you used to hang around... They ain't hatin' on us 'cause they're white, they're hatin' 'cause their daddy is the devil. And the devil will use any trap or rebellion... But, just so happens around here, he likes to use hate and color to drag souls down to hell."

"Why do we have to live here? Why do we have to deal with all their hate, Daddy?"

"I done told you, Betty," he answered sharply. "This is our home, and this is God's dream to our family. Hate is everywhere... ain't no place in this messed-up world that's void of hate. No matter where you go, you got hate. We just got Jimmy and Billy's hate here." He smiled to console me. "'Sides that, how're people like Jimmy and Billy gonna' get right with God, if they don't have all of us to show them themselves?"

Daddy stopped smiling and took a long, deep breath. He could see my concern. I didn't tell him about the episodes of white men who came home from work early, knowing I was still cleaning... knowing their wives were gone. And how they would grin, talk nicely, and rub up against me while passing. And how a few even tried to grab me… and how my squirming mixed with my 'Your wife due home any minute' shouts had made my narrow escapes… so far. I didn't tell Daddy about a lot of things.

But he could see it all in my eyes…

"Betty, we gonna' be outta' here when the time is right," he said softly. "You need help, you come to me. I ain't gonna' let nothin' happen to y'all. But Doctor King got it right in his fight. Only love can destroy hate, and only integration can get us ready for heaven… You have to trust me. You have to trust God. I know it looks sometimes like He abandoned us. But He ain't left us, and He ain't goin' to."

"Thanks, Daddy," I said.

I recalled what the Lord had spoken to me years ago, as I walked away. "We're being divided… permanently," I muttered. "Nothing here gonna' last nohow like Daddy said…"

Segregation versus integration. Fighting for our equal rights versus separating ourselves. But it seemed we couldn't be separated peacefully in America. *'Was this really the land of our enemies, as the bible insinuated?'* I wondered. When people don't want peace, no matter what you do, it surely seems that way.

My faded dreams sometimes rose back into the spotlight…

Either way, the civil rights era was an exhilarating time. The fight was on! Hate-filled people had their temporal victories, of course. However, slowly but surely, the nonviolent ways of Christ began to catch up and surpass them. All over the country, there came victories and losses on the nightly news. At times, I stopped watching the Hollywood movies and other entertainment to keep a tally of them.

These national changes of growth, entertainment, and recreation eventually made their own way into our little town of Cameron,

Missouri. There was a lot of talk among the people and articles in the newspaper about a new golf course, a new swimming pool, and a brand-new city park. It would be "top of the line", I heard them say. I heard Daddy and Mamma talking about it nearly every evening when I got home.

For me, personally, I could barely keep up with all the happenings. When the white homeowners left me to myself, which was almost all the time, I could do my job, praise God, and then sit down anxiously to watch the daily newscasts about the civil rights and other news unique to the era. I have to admit that I would still watch some of the wonderful movies on the television or listen to the latest new music on the radio. Once in a while, I would even settle in for what the white people called "soaps", but the black people referred to them as "stories".

When they were home, several white housewives would even invite me to sit down with them. We would watch intently while sipping tea. For the whites I was around, entertainment became the epitome of American culture. It became bigger than work, going outdoors, and even having conversations. More and more, people became glued to their televisions or were dancing to their radios. For most black folks in the '50's, economic conditions kept us from too much television, dancing, or even keeping up with the Civil Rights movement. Work still had to come first.

One night, after a long day at work, Daddy handed me a letter. It was from Henry. I rarely got mail with my name on it. I excitedly dropped my things and ran to my room where I could read it peacefully and privately. My heart pounded as I ripped open the envelope and read:

Dear Betty,

The Lord impressed on me to write you an urgent message... Do not take this lightly. I know the Lord speaks to you and will confirm this...

You have, no doubt, been seeing and experiencing all the changes that have been going on in our country. With all your temptation to participate in a white world, which was attained through murdering our People, I send you a warning.

The Children of Israel have no business enjoying all the wicked pleasures of Babylon. When they do, they are playing THEIR games, living THEIR prosperity, living THEIR dreams, and serving THEIR gods. These gods will surely lead to destruction.

Like the local moonshine, it will feel good for a moment, but it will eventually kill you after taking you out of your created and intended state. It will steal your soul forever...

In America, we are intrinsically sabotaged after our hearts become like the enemy's. Then blacks turn against blacks. When this happens, then we have an even greater level of evil to contend with. The bible says, "By faith, Moses, when he was grown up, refused to be called the son of Pharaoh's daughter, choosing rather to be mistreated with the People of God than to enjoy the fleeting pleasures of sin."

Be like Moses, Betty. Choose God's latter rewards instead of today's ill-gotten treasure. In doing, you will have God today and tomorrow.

Why do we, as a People, want what he has? Our Father will give us much more than temporal prosperity.

Seek God and justice always. Seek equality, but know that it is our Lord that will bring his People to the promise land. Do not grow jealous or participate in sin. Our God will give us much more than this, coupled with compassion. We don't have to sell our souls. Don't lose your heart. Guard your soul. Walk holy. Stay true to our Father. I don't think I will be around much longer; but know that I will never forget our brief time and conversations together.

Your friend, Henry

That summer of 1958, Henry was murdered by a white mob in Texas. Like Malcolm X, who would be assassinated on February 21, 1965, and Dr. Martin Luther King, who would also be killed on April 4, 1968, Henry joined them in dying for what he believed. There were, and would later be, thousands of men and women, whose names were never known but by their loved ones and God, whose names were never recorded in history books, who would, nevertheless, give the ultimate sacrifice of their very lives, their very being, for others' rights.

I would later find out that Henry had been working in his spare time for the black Texas sharecroppers, whose partial or entire profits were being stolen illegally by corruption. He died defending the defenseless, being a voice for the oppressed. How I would have loved to tell him to be careful or to back off at times. But he couldn't help it. Henry fulfilled his purpose. He had made his choice as the crucified thief. Instead of choosing prosperity and safety, he died. He died to stand for righteousness. And I know he's happy now.

I can recall the day that Daddy told me about Henry's death. I guess he thought that I might be distraught, but I smiled instead. I smiled for the life of Henry. Henry, my friend...

Daddy seemed to understand, and he smiled, too.

I turned and made my way into the bathroom and shut the door. I looked carefully at myself in the mirror for several, long minutes. Then slowly, I let down my hair. Determinedly, I wiped away the fake mole that replicated Marilyn Monroe. I carefully removed the large earrings of Ruby Dee and tossed them into the trash. And I even pressed away the thick lipstick of Ella Fitzgerald.

... Like a butterfly. Softly... gently... I flew.

Something Daddy had said echoed in my mind, as I continued to stare in the mirror. He told me that God had made an entire nation powerful because of one believer... because of a single dream... Joseph's dream from God had transformed the destiny of an entire People.

I secretly wondered if God could... would... change circumstances based on my dreams...

I looked at myself carefully, my real self...

... And I liked her.

14

"Right in the Way of Satan"

The cold winter winds began to blow across the plains of Northwest Missouri. All day and into the evening, until Daddy came in to lay down his tired bones, there was still arguing of some form in our home. Instead of feeling trust and protection, sometimes it felt as if we legitimately began to despise one another. I can recall, many evenings, walking in amongst the yelling, giving a quick wave, and heading to my bed. I grabbed a bowl of whatever was cooking in the kitchen, sat down, and listened to the latest dispute. But more recently, rather than to eat at home, I would grab a bite offered to me at the last home I cleaned or grab any kind of anything that would fill me at the local drugstore on the way home, just to avoid hearing the chaos. I didn't want to partake in foolishness. I just wanted enough sleep to get up and go do my job again the next day.

The words in Henry's warning were coming true… *"In America, it is intrinsically sabotaged, after our hearts become like the enemy's. Then blacks turn against blacks. When this happens, then we have Satan, his devils, AND each other to contend with."* Though I saw it all happening right in front of my eyes, I didn't know how to stop it. It was as though many of us believed the negative verbal assaults tossed at our race. It was as if we hated ourselves. It was as if we had become what THEY said we were. We wanted to thrive, we longed to survive, but we began to slowly hate ourselves at the same time.

Evil schemes had taken their intended toll on weary souls. And I know the devils grinned with delight as they witnessed their deceptive schemes at work.

"Girl, your hair looks crazy today," Ephraim might yell out at June. "Put some oil in that nest!"

"Just as soon as you change your stinkin' underwear," June would scream back.

At night, I began to have a recurring dream. In the dream, I was walking up the dusty road of Cameron that led away from our house. Out of nowhere, a tiny snake suddenly bit my heel. At that moment, I kept walking as if nothing had happened at all. But, as I fully grasped the notion that an actual snake had just bit me in the heel, I thought that I had better go home and get it examined by Mamma or Daddy. However, as I approached my home, I stopped in my tracks. There were snakes everywhere! Snakes of all sizes, entwined with each other, surrounded our entire home. And then I would wake up, not knowing what the dream meant.

This same dream would continue at least three or four times a week... I knew from past dreams and visions, that the presence of snakes in my dreams meant nothing good. As a matter of fact, it would seem that surely something bad was about to happen. But why were the snakes at our house? And why were there so many? I didn't have an answer...

But I knew that verbal battles opened the doors of hell. When I wasn't having the dreams about snakes, another dream, would surface. I would see myself asleep, and then actually have a vision, within the dream, of a woman carrying a little baby. But this baby didn't have a face. There was just a faceless void, though everything else about the baby was normal. Again, I didn't understand. But this vision of the faceless baby had been barging into my unconsciousness since I was a child. I didn't know who the baby was. I only knew that the baby with the invisible face scared me.

Later, the God of heaven would reveal the meaning of this dream. The faceless baby was the missing identity of His people. For the most part, many of us didn't know that we were the Hebrews of the bible.

Every other race knew their origin, their country, their ethnicity, their roots… Like the prophecy, our identity had been hidden from us. Maybe that's why we fight and kill one another… If we only knew who we were!

But, for now, the meaning of this dream was hidden from me. As soon as I would awake, I would quickly put these dreams out of my mind. I had enough to do, and enough to worry about. Daddy was getting older, and twelve people were now living in our home. I would give Mamma a third of my pay every week, stash a third into savings, and use the other third to live and buy things I needed. I figured, one day, when the time was right, when the right man shows up, I want to be able to move into our own home. I was now doing what I could to plan for my future.

Something else was continuing to happen in our community. The Cameron City Planning Committee was promoting their "state of the art" swimming facility, city park, and golf course. Their plans were now fully coming into fruition. It seemed that they now had the full support of the community, the funds to build, and the property chosen.

There was only one problem. The property they chose came right up to our back door. And, it seemed, the plans included buying and tearing down our home. We were right in the way of their plans.

I would come home after another long day, and, almost nightly, I would hear men outside talking emphatically to Daddy. They had been calm and friendly at first with a "Well, Joshua, you just think about our offer, and we'll get back to you," conclusion to their first several conversations.

These "polite" offers lasted about two weeks. The offer was to move our family out to the country. There we would be given the same amount of land, the same size home, and "maybe an acre or two extra for Daddy's trouble".

I would hear Mamma and Daddy discussing it well into the night...

"I don't want to move, Joshua," I would hear Mamma whisper. "We're out far enough. I like it where we are. I don't want to go out to the country where nobody is."

Daddy would always mutter the same thing in his "not-so-quiet" grumbling... "I don't trust 'em, Sarina," he would say. "White folks are always promising things that they never deliver on... I don't trust 'em... I know somewhere they're gonna' short us and hang us out to dry..."

"We worked hard to get this home just the way we like it," Mamma would then point out, referring to the many repairs made on the house, or something that was close to being finished. "I don't want to start all over again..."

"They stick us out there, Sarina, where nobody is?" Daddy would then conjecture. "Next thing you know, 'ol Jimmy and his KKK be makin' sport of us. And no one around to see 'em..." Then Daddy would walk over and tap on the fireplace, which he always did when he was nervous. "Hell, nah, Sarina... I don't trust 'em..."

Night after night, I would hear these same type of reckonings at the kitchen table, until Daddy would end the discussion with, "Well, nothin' we can do tonight 'bout it... Let's turn in..."

But soon the city planners became much more aggressive with their approach. I would come home from work and see men arguing with Daddy in the front yard. But Daddy was stubborn. He didn't get to where he was by being foolish or passive.

"We ain't goin' nowhere," Joshua would finally say. "And that's that!"

But the city planners were also just as intent to carry out their own plans. I would hear them offering things like cars, cash, and more land. Sometimes I would sit on the front porch and snicker as the offers got more interesting. At one point, a frustrated man blurted out, mocking Daddy, "We'll see if we can get you two homes and four cars, Joshua!"

"Y'all know you can't get that," Daddy yelled. "I done heard your offers. One broken-down home and zero cars way out yonder is your real deal. And I don't even trust that. The answer is no."

At times, Jimmy and Billy would slowly drive by, after hearing through the grapevine that no deal was made and that maybe a little intimidation might help Joshua along. They would watch from a distance just close enough to hear. Each of them would get out of the police car, lean against a nearby tree, smoking and chewing while glaring at Daddy as he argued with the developers. But no doubt, Daddy never gave in. Finally, Daddy would throw his hands upward out of frustration while walking back into the house.

I would watch carefully as the men walked off. Not caring that I was still sitting and listening to them, they would mutter things like, "These darkies are right in the way of the plans... We've got to figure out how to get them out of here..."

I would sit outside watching men coming, walking around our property who were total strangers carrying their rolled-up plans, as they lay them carefully on the ground discussing things. They would completely ignore me as if I was invisible.

To all those men, we were not people, and this was not a family home... We were simply problems in the way of their progress, obstacles in the way of profits and visions. And, if there's one thing I've seen in America, problems are dealt with and obstacles are destroyed... If the problems are in the form of black people, it's the people who are expendable. A simple change of plans, in the hands of elitists, are not even considered.

As Daddy reached the point where he refused to talk to the men any longer, that's when they suddenly decided to switch tactics...

"Good evening, Joshua," a man greeted, walking up to the front porch. This was someone whom we had never seen before.

It was the late Fall of 1958. This man came all alone. He grinned a mischievous smile while kicking into the fracture of our broken sidewalk that led up to the house. He wore nice business clothes, but on his head was the hard, yellow hat of a construction worker.

"What is it this time?" Daddy glanced up from cleaning his work boots. "I told y'all I'm done talkin' about this movin' stuff. We're stayin' right here, case you didn't get the word."

"Well, Joshua, I don't agree with all the animosity that's come against your fine family," the man said politely. "My name is Brian Winters, and I'm the lead foreman of this project for this fine town... Its swimming pool and new golf course will be excellent and prosperous additions..."

"Where're you from?" Daddy interrupted.

"Our firm is out of Topeka, Kansas," the man said. He pierced his mouth slightly, letting Daddy know that he didn't appreciate being interrupted. But then he continued to talk. "The way I see it, Joshua..."

"My name is Mr. Jackson," Daddy interrupted again. "I don't know you. My name is Mr. Jackson, and I run the trash disposal service up here." He looked up and eyeballed the man carefully.

"My job is to run all the garbage out of this town," implying an indirect insult.

The man's smile disappeared. "Look, Mr. Jackson, I want to help you…"

"Help me with what?" Daddy smirked. "What offer you got for me to move today?"

"Well, that's just it," the man answered politely. "We don't want to move you. We want to help you to stay right here where you are happy."

"We don't need help with that," Daddy abruptly replied. "We don't need your help to change what's already here. Thank you for letting us stay… You can go now."

Mr. Winters took a deep breath while sizing up Joshua. He could tell that Daddy had no fear. He proceeded carefully. "Well, I've suggested a slight compromise, certain terms with the city of Cameron, in order to keep you here," he said. "May I sit down?"

"No," Daddy answered. "No need to sit and no need to compromise. We're fine right here."

"But this compromise is one where you can't lose," he countered. "We want to make better on your home here and fix it up… Free of charge, of course…"

"Why?" Joshua frowned.

"Well, that's the compromise," the man answered. "If you want to stay, we want you to have the finest-looking home in town. We want a model home to sit next to our new project."

"I can fix my own home," Daddy said, turning and slowly walking back toward the house. He didn't trust anyone involved.

"That will cost you hundreds, if not thousands of dollars, Joshua… um, Mr. Jackson."

He recognized Daddy's slight hesitation and pounced on this new crack of opportunity.

"We would re-do your home by putting our brand new, custom-fitted, designed siding on your home... completely free. I can tell that you are a businessman, Mr. Jackson, and this is a good deal. If you and your lovely family want to stay, we want your home to beautify the area. We want your home to have the finest look in Cameron. It's a win-win for you. You get to stay, and you get an updated home!"

Daddy knew that the house needed a paint job, new porch and the cracks repaired on the sidewalk. A project he wasn't looking forward to next Spring... especially at his age...

"I want new shutters on every window," Daddy said with a sudden change in tone.

"Done!" the man exclaimed.

"And... and... the roof has a couple of places that could use patching..."

"We'll put new shingles on your entire roof too," he said, as he pushed his voice on heavily so Joshua would hear him. "We want your home to be completely stunning for folks to look at!"

Daddy gave the man a long, hard look as if to say, 'Okay, no games... I'm trusting you to do this right...'

"When you want to get started?" Joshua asked softly. "Gonna' be getting' cold soon..."

"How about Monday?"

Daddy stretched out his rough, stained hand. "Okay, I'll shake on it!"

"I promise you won't be sorry, Mr. Jackson," the foreman said smoothly, accepting Joshua's huge hand. "We'll make things work perfectly."

191

Monday morning, bright and early, even before I left for work, a crew of men with three trucks showed up as promised. A few of the men smiled at me flirtatiously, as I walked away. I knew they were watching so I exhibited my sexiest stroll. I heard whispering and dainty comments from a couple of the men behind me and the word "chocolate". I didn't turn around.

I made it a point to arrive home earlier than normal that evening to see what the men had done to the house. The sun had just set, but there was still plenty of light to see that the home was beautifully different. The house was painted with some kind of greenish-gray color that I had never seen before on any other home. The roof and new shutters shined with a new tint of sparkling black. The clean windows reflected the colors of the sky. Overall, I had never seen our home look so nice. It looked like something right out of a white folks' magazine. The front porch had been repaired and the cracks on the walkway filled.

Daddy sat on the porch with a smile on his face. "I got them to do everything, Betty," he said proudly. "See what can happen when you stick to your guns?"

I felt an uneasiness. White niceness, especially free white niceness, always had a catch someplace. But I didn't want to spoil Daddy's feeling after a victorious day. After all, victories for a black man were rare in 1958. I felt genuinely happy for Daddy Joshua. He always did his best to look out for his family.

There was no way I was going to ruin this moment on this beautiful Fall evening.

"You did it, Daddy," I smiled, watching him light up his pipe like a king. "The home looks wonderful! Let me know when *"Better Homes and Gardens"* comes to take pictures!"

"Haaaaaaaaaaaaa," Daddy whooped.

I hadn't heard that sound in a while. I dismissed the negative thoughts that wanted to creep back into my heart and mind. Maybe that businessman had been telling the truth. Maybe Cameron just didn't want to have an eyesore of a house next to their glorious, new golf links... I doubted it, but how could this go wrong? The Spirit seemed to want to speak in His "still, quiet" way, but I was tired. I focused on getting into bed early that night in our "new" home.

That night, I had a different dream... one that I had never had before.

In it, I heard lots of people coming, similar to my past dream where a Hebrew army of people came powerfully into view. But, when these masses came over the hill, they were a different type of men. Some of them reminded me of the same men trying to get Daddy to sell the home. They didn't march, they weren't orderly and disciplined. No, these people just walked with an informal gait. Some had women with them, some were laughing and joking, some were sad, but most of them had indifferent, robotic expressions. And they kept coming and coming, males and females, old and young, lines and lines of people, all moving in the same direction towards an unspecified destination. As I looked into the horizon, watching the thousands, maybe even millions, of an unwitting type of people coming from the distance, the dream suddenly turned ghastly. Suddenly, I could hear screams of anxiety and terror!

I turned to see what all the turmoil was, and I watched in frozen fear at the horrendous sight that I was now witnessing. The lines upon lines of people, oppressors, approached a cliff to a bottomless, black pit...

Without control, they suddenly spotted their fate. And, as terror seized their hearts, one by one, they were reeled forever into the vacuum of heat and darkness. It was so real. The dream testified. It was so scary, so hellish, so... so final!

Some of them tried to resist, but there was no stopping their physical momentum, as if an invisible force was pushing them forward, then sucking them in. I couldn't tell what the force was. I just watched their faces, distressed and petrified. None of them even suspected what was coming, as the huge, smoking hole closed and reopened to receive the group in front of them. Some twisted and clawed the air, but there was nothing they could do.

I wanted to wake up. This dream was, by far, the most terrifying one that I had ever experienced. I stared in shock, forced to watch the thousands, even millions, walking calmly towards a gruesome death. Even worse, I knew that this wasn't only death… It was never-ending, never-again-a-second-of-sympathy, relentless torment. Their fear and pain will never diminish one iota.

God spoke to me in dream. Not one second of relief or comfort… Forever…

They would never again experience any form of light, any form of water, any kind of a cool breeze, any form of rest or relaxation, any form of love, or even a deep, calm breath. Every form of mercy was gone.

In life, when mercy should have been given, they gave none. And now… None would be given.

The most deafening screams I had ever heard echoed from those who went over the edge, their arms and legs flailing as they hurled and then disappeared into the deep, deep abyss.

I rarely feel anything in my dreams that would make me wake up screaming, but…

My eyes popped open with a loud scream already coming out of my gut. I sat up to see June, Esther, James, and little Tony looking at me. The morning light peaked in from a slightly-torn window shade.

"You okay?" James blurted out.

Daddy came running in with his gun. "What's going on in here?"

I threw my body back down onto the bed, embarrassed. "Sorry," I said groggily. "It was a dream..."

"Jesus, I thought a spider bit you," June said, turning over to go back to sleep.

I stared at the ceiling, my heart still pounding with fright. Long after everyone had gotten up and walked out of the bedroom, I stayed there, trying to shake the fear of the dream. I closed my eyes, took a deep breath, and silently thanked God that it was only a dream.

After several minutes, my fear turned into curiosity. Was this dream true? Were there really that many people being hurled into the abyss of hell? God have mercy... Why?

Tears began to fall down my cheeks. I covered my face with the bed sheet in case anyone walked in. I replayed the scene of the violent destinies in my mind. 'I wouldn't want this end for anyone,' I thought. 'Not even my worst enemy'. What should I do? I imagined myself telling Jimmy and Billy, and trying to lead them to Christ...

"Why, Lord?" I asked out loud.

Just then, He reminded me of the sighting that Evelyn June had seen just one week before mine, because she, too, had dreams and visions, and saw real creatures of the night.

In the vision, June was sleeping and suddenly heard some whistling in the backyard close to where Daddy kept his pigs. Looking out the bedroom window she could see a man's face, but it also looked similar to the face of a goat. This creature was standing upward on two hind legs, a hideous picture of a creature from the underworld. Frightened, she quickly lay back in the bed, and pulled the covers tightly over her head. But as she lay there, she wondered... 'Where did it go? Is it still out there?'

Now the whistling had stopped. 'I'll just peek slightly over the covers to see where it went,' June had thought. So slowly June lifted down the covers..., but to her fright, BOOM!!! There it was, the creature staring down directly into her face. She gasped for air, as she noticed the horns on top of his head. June quickly pulled the covers back over her head, shivering... never to come out again until the morning light.

June said it was real. She had told me that night, that cold winter night, that that sighting would change our lives at home forever.

Fresh off my dream, and recalling June's vision, my heart began to pound again. Just then Mamma walked in, gathering up all the laundry.

"What you doin', Betty?" she asked with concern. "Ain't you goin' to work today? Are you sick?"

"I'm getting up, Mamma," I said, my face still crushed into the pillow. "Just had a bad dream, that's all..."

"Hmmm," she said talking to herself. "Our family has always had those dreams. It can be a burden at times... But they're always true. People don't want to hear it, and you might even try to second-guess them your own self... But they're always true..."

Mamma disappeared out the door. She mostly moved fast, all day, every day...

My late start had taken a toll on my day. I still made it to the three homes I was scheduled to clean that day, but I didn't have the time to watch any of the "stories" or civil rights news. I had to work extra hard, extra fast, to make up the time. After all, if you didn't finish your work before leaving, some of those white folks wouldn't even pay you... not even a partial amount!

As I worked, I would, at times, think about the faces and the screams of those people, as they felt themselves leaving the comforts and light of this world for the very last time. At those moments, I froze with temporary anxiety and grief.

At one of my frozen moments, Mrs. Turner walked into the room I was cleaning. She was looking for something. She had a cigarette in one hand and a small glass of bourbon in the other. She found the magazine she'd been looking for and glanced up to see me staring at the wall with a vase in my hand I'd been dusting.

"Try to keep moving, Betty," she said, before switching on the light near the doorway. "We have a dinner party tomorrow, and it's getting late."

"Yes, ma'am," I said, in a humble voice I had used hundreds of times to appease my white employers. A 'yes, ma'am' or 'certainly, sir' could work wonders, even with the most petulant of clients, if said in the right fashion. It satisfied even the most demanding.

That night, returning from work, I slowly approached our home noticing the night sky over our home. It sat more darkly than usual. It seemed that a streetlight, maybe even two, had burned out before the evening.

I was home so late that everyone was sleeping. I crept in and grabbed a bowl of stew in the refrigerator. I heard Ephraim snoring loudly. I didn't worry about heating my food. I broke off a piece of bread out of the loaf inside the bread box and took my food to the front porch. It was winter now.

The fresh coat of paint on the house from the city workers agreement had already began peeling and falling off the house into the snow that was still on the ground from a couple of days ago. The air was getting colder by the minute, but it wasn't too bad for December.

As I sat down and ate with my coat on, I thought I heard a few noises in the distance... probably the local raccoons. But the night was so dark... it was eerie. I quickly swallowed my food, said a quick prayer that I wouldn't have any dreams this night, got up, and started to walk back inside.

I heard another noise.

"You 'coons better get on outta' here," I turned and yelled, just like the store owners often did to me and my sister June when white customers were shopping. And, like the raccoons, we would run out obediently in fear for our lives.

I took one last gaze around the dark perimeters outside. The only movement was the stream of steam that came from my breathing. I snuck back inside and locked the door.

There were all twelve of us in the house on that December night in 1958. In one bedroom was Daddy and Mamma.., 12-year-old Lawrence, 11-year-old Joshua, Jr., and 9-year-old Everett Francis, better known as Butchy, slept in another room. In the upstairs bedroom was Esther and James, and their baby we called Little Tony., 15-year-old Evelyn June and myself slept in the living room. 18-year-old Ephraim slumbered on a cot in the kitchen. And 23-year-old Dan was in the room Daddy had built onto the house for a pantry.

When you work late sometimes and share a home with twelve people, you learn how to disrobe quietly. I lay my clothes next to the bed, took my nylon slip from under the hay mattress, and put it on. As I lay down, careful not to disturb June, I began to grow anxious about the possible things God might show me tonight in my sleep.

Little did I know, this night would be much, much worse than any dreams the Lord had ever given me. God prepares us to handle the most gruesome of tragedies. But He doesn't always let us know when they're coming. My worry would have been much greater had I known what the devil had in store for us this night. But, instead, my fatigued body let the medicine of sleep slowly induce its tranquilizing effects.

I fell into a deep sleep.

15

"The Fire"

S uddenly, I awoke when I heard a loud scream echoing through the hallway. It was Ephraim. But was this real? Was I hearing what I was hearing... or was it the horrible screams like in the dream the night before? I hesitated for just an instant. Then I heard Ephraim yelling again. "Ohhh, no..." he screamed. "My God! Fire!!! Everyone wake up!!! Y'all get out of here!" A piece of cloth from a curtain on fire had fallen on his ear, burning him. "Get up!" he screamed again.

But it was too late. I saw the fires of Hell everywhere throughout the house. I sat up, startled from the loud screams and the increasing heat. Within seconds, the bedroom was filled with flames. I could feel the unbearable heat coming from the aggressiveness of the fire, as it ripped throughout the house from room to room, snapping, destroying, and polarizing everything in its path.

I was naked. In the middle of the night, I must have taken off my nylon slip to avoid being hot.

Why wasn't anyone else in our home awake? And how was this fire spreading so quickly? Our bed was only about fifteen feet from the room Daddy had built where my brother Dan was sleeping. I remember that terrifying scream that came from Ephraim. At first, I didn't see the flames, I only heard them. But the inside of the room... It was now glowing bright red. The heat was so hot, it felt like someone had thrown me right inside of an oven!

"Fire! Fire!" I heard Ephraim continue to shout with panic.

The heat was quickly becoming even more extreme. The hay beds began to catch fire from sparks dripping through the ceiling. Even the walls and ceiling glowed a strange red of curling, fiendish heat. The face of the devil appeared out of the twisting ceiling. He was grinning. Other demons seemed to appear with him. But I didn't have time for them. I glanced next to me, where Evelyn June was sound asleep.

"June, get up!" I shouted.

Evelyn barely moved as I violently shook her. How could she sleep so soundly? Finally, I turned and forcefully gave her a hard shove. I knocked her out of the bed and onto the floor.

Someone had opened the door, or maybe it was the window. I don't know... But when they did, the flames came in like huge, long fingers attacking us. June and I whirled in confusion.

"Which way is out?" June cried bitterly.

Black smoke now caused us both to be even more disoriented. I wasn't sure which family members had escaped the flames running out first, but I knew I had to help Evelyn. I reached back through the smolder to find her, moving my arms around quickly into the empty spaces of the room. The air draft now coming in from the outside enhanced the flames around us.

Finally, I found her and shoved her out of the bedroom, as she dug her fingernails into my skin. Panicking, all she could do was look around at the flames of fire everywhere. The front door was our only way out. I squeezed Evelyn's shoulder as I thrust her towards the front door. Filled with fear, she didn't want to move. The closer we got to the door, the hotter the fire grew. I planned what was our only hope. I braced myself for one quick dash, but Evelyn June wasn't cooperating.

I looked into her eyes, declared an unspoken word of aspiration, and, before she could resist again, I pushed her through the flames, out the door, and onto the top of the snowbank.

With Evelyn's hair flaming, along with the clothes on her back burning, she dipped her head in the snow to put out the fire. Mamma was already outside, and she ran over quickly to stop the flames that were still smoldering on June's back. Her back resembled pieces of coal still simmering from the heat. Her pain was so great, Mamma watched Evelyn open her mouth, but nothing came out.

But I was still stuck in the house. The flames were now ready to swallow me up alive. I had disappeared behind a wall of fire, surrendering to the reality that I would never see the light of day again.

It was at that moment, where I didn't scream, and I couldn't move... I could only stand there hopelessly tormented in the immersion of burning flames...

The pain became intolerable beyond death. I prepared to die... This was to be my fateful end...

'*Please take me quickly*', I thought... '*I want to die quickly!*'.

But then I felt Them... They felt like giant, powerful Hands. These Hands held me still so that I couldn't move, gripping my body as I surrendered to the thought of being burned alive. There was still the pain, but now I didn't panic. It was as if everything was moving in slow motion. My whole life flashed before my eyes. Mamma, Daddy, all the good times we had, even in our disagreements; my siblings, the love we all shared.

The seconds lingered in judgment... I closed my eyes. Was I in hell? But I heard the screams of Joshua, Jr. and Butch in the other room to my right. I realized then that I was still in the house. There was no one around in the room, only fire... And then I asked God, so calmly, so vividly... "What did I do that You would burn me alive, Lord?"

At that very moment I felt another huge Hand pressing into my back. I cannot adequately describe what happened next. But what happened was extraordinary! Something, Someone took control. I clearly felt a pull, and the Hands held me no longer, propelling me out of the flames and onto the front porch. Thrashing violently, I collapsed.

I can't tell you how I was able to survive. I didn't realize that I was on fire. As I tried to get up to make my way towards the snow, parts of the flaming roof from the porch fell on my back, knocking me back down. Daddy, along with two of my big brothers, quickly ran over to help me.

Somehow, I had been released and pushed by an invisible... Force. I knew that the Hands belonged to God Himself... or maybe they were those of an angel on assignment. Regardless, although I had resigned to my death, He had other ideas. He had other plans for my life. He determined that it wasn't yet my time.

As I continued my inconceivable inertia outside, I realized that God had rescued me in just enough time to keep me from being captured by the flames. Although momentarily trapped under the falling porch, it didn't stop my momentum. I bounced up with the help of my brothers, then suddenly fainted into my daddy's arms. He laid me a safe distance away from the house.

Despite my desire to remain unconscious, my mind had other ideas. More pain shot through me, as my burnt body sizzled from the heat... Yes, an actual sizzling, like a piece of meat off the grill... still simmering.

I now lay naked, face down in the snow, my skin hanging off my bones like shoestrings, my flesh like burnt ribbons...

The first person I saw when I looked up was Lawrence. He was kneeling down in the yard looking helpless and scared. Local Cameron people were already gathering outside. Mamma, who had grabbed Evelyn June and told her to dip her head in the snow, pressed her head into the snow again to put out the fire that was still smoldering in her hair. My own hair had completely burned off my head, though I didn't know it yet. I was completely bald.

I turned the other direction and saw Mamma who had now moved. She was in Daddy's arms, but leaning towards the house, hollering out, "My babies!!" Then there was a loud crash, as I heard the entire house fall violently...

Someone put a piece of clothing on me to cover my naked body. I heard sirens in the background, between the frightened voices of nearby neighbors that drowned them out. As I opened and closed my eyes, I saw a strange sight... The snow on the ground continued to burn... The metal fence along our property was even rolling in flames. How could snow and metal fencing continue to burn with fire?

Then I thought I heard... laughter. Surely it couldn't be... I heard it again... unmistakable, slightly-muffled laughter... And, as I squinted in that direction, there I saw Jimmy and Billy in the distance... actually smiling... It was too much to bear... I blacked out...

Unfortunately, three members of my family were burned alive in the fast-moving flames that night... Joshua, Jr., Everett Francis, better known as Butchy... and Esther and James' little baby, James Anthony, better known as Little Tony.

I later found out from my sister just how little Tony died. He was only a little over a year old. Esther said that she and her husband James were upstairs sleeping.

Dashing up quickly to head for the window, and not remembering that the window had been boarded up for the winter, Esther grabbed little Tony first. But then, for a moment, decided to set him down to knock open the window. After getting the window open, turning and then reaching back to rescue little Tony, he had disappeared into the flames. He had crawled off, perhaps into another room, and they couldn't find him. In their half-conscious, panicked state, they had lost him , and little Tony burned to death in the quick-moving flames.

Another story was that Joshua, Jr. and Butchy couldn't see to find their way out. Either way, we lost our littlest loved ones in the house and that was a tragedy. It left a hole in our hearts forever...

After helping June and I, Daddy had tried his best to go back in. He desperately tried to look for the three boys the best he could. But he couldn't find them. They had probably gone the wrong direction and were quickly trapped. Shortly afterwards, the entire house fell.

I periodically came back to consciousness. But, when the pain hit, I fainted again...

And Daddy, like me, eventually passed out in the yard after the house fell.

Mamma slumped to her knees, her arms stretched out, her palms helplessly facing upward... she screamed. Her only response, her only prayer, was just a piercing, primal cry... She had finally gotten over the death of George. And now this. A tragedy she would never get over. She would go into a state of deep depression for nearly a year... not because of her injuries, but due to her broken heart and mental grief.

I woke up. Dan was helping me to my feet and into the car, because an ambulance had not arrived yet. "I'll take you to the hospital," was all I heard him say. I could feel my bones sticking to the back of the car's seat.

"Where's Evelyn June?" I asked. But no one answered me.

White people, some that I recognized, some I didn't, only stared at me through their car windows, as they rode by wondering what happened. I gazed shamefully back at them and slowly lowered my head, before looking back. There was Evelyn June. I spotted her and Daddy still sprawled out on the ground. I didn't know if they were dead or alive at the time. Mamma still screamed. The snowy ground was still burning with fire even after the house collapsed. 'How strange,' I remember thinking again... 'Snow that burns with fire.'

Our home was just a large pile of ash now. You couldn't tell that it had ever been a home at all.

When we finally arrived at the hospital, it was 4:30 in the morning. The doctors and surgeons were called in. I wanted a drink of water so badly. My throat was scorched and burning. But the nurses wouldn't give me any.

"You're going to have to wait until we give you an anesthetic," one of them said.

As I went in and out of consciousness, I saw several hospital workers place Evelyn in a bed next to mine. *'Thank you God'*, I thought. June is still alive.

I woke up temporarily and saw a doctor walk in. He must have thought that we were both unconscious as he dropped his head and said to the nurse in the room, "These two aren't going to make it," before walking out.

Afterwards, a couple of nurses then put a big, white screen up between us, so that one of us would not be able to see the other one die.

I could only think of two prayers at that moment; the Lord's Prayer and the 23rd Psalm, that I had learned in school from Miss Ridge. I repeated the verses over and over again the best I could. Whenever I reached the part in the 23rd Psalm that says, "Though I walk through the valley of the shadow of death...", I placed Evelyn June's name in the prayer.

"Though June walks through the valley of the shadow of death, June shall fear no evil," I said as loud as I could. "... For Thou art with June; Thy rod and Thy staff comfort June..."

When I was done, I called for her.

"June..."

No answer.

"June!"

But still no answer.

I thought, 'Either June was dead or asleep'. The nurses gave me no hints.

I tried my best to fall asleep.

This cycle continued several days... Pain, prayer, ask for June, sleep...

One afternoon, I awoke to see a nurse putting more anesthetic in the clear bag hanging next to my bed. I looked around her to see a man standing in the doorway. I felt so uncomfortable as the man stood there staring. He was not even blinking. He didn't look at me with compassion or have any kind of expression. He uniquely focused on me and stared at me indifferently. It was as though he was dissecting my thoughts, my state of condition. What was he thinking? The nurse glanced over and saw me watching him. She turned and looked.

"May I help you sir?" she asked.

Ignoring her, he continued to stare insistently, awkwardly at me, from the doorway.

The nurse walked over and slammed the door in his face. "Creep," she muttered.

Then I fell back asleep. I wasn't ready for the bodily pain that these days and weeks would bring. When the nurses changed our bandages, our skin was freshly ripped off of our aching bodies. The only slight break from the agony would be enough painkillers to put us to sleep again. And, when sleep finally moved upon us, we didn't know if we would ever wake again.

A doctor would come in at times and give a negative report for our future.

"Well, still hanging on, I see," one after another would say politely, whenever they saw I was conscious.

Then I would hear them mutter something like "Probably not for long though…"

After writing something down on a chart, each doctor would shake his head, turn around, give a nod to the nurse, and then walk out. Some doctors would look at me like a science project and comment, "Wow, never saw anyone live through these burns…" It was heartless. Not even a, 'Hope you get better, Betty'. I've heard better bedside manners for a dying dog at a vet.

But, again, the people who were disciples of Christ, I could tell, because they spoke differently than the doctors.

Daddy's sister, Aunt Lizzy, would come in the room but wouldn't talk to me. She would speak directly to my body…

"Peace, body," she would repeat for several minutes.

I tried to speak to Aunt Lizzy.

"Hush, now, Betty," she would shush me. "I'm talkin' to your body."

I started to cry.

"Shut up," Aunt Lizzy would say to me. "Quiet, now."

"Body?" she ordered. "I know you hear me, body… Peace, now… Peace, body!"

Strangely, my body actually responded to her voice. I felt a sensation like smooth ointment as she continued with her, "Peace, body, in Yeshua's Name." I was so grateful. Strangely Aunt Lizzy was one of our only family members that used the name Yeshua.

The prayers from Aunt Lizzy and others put me to sleep gracefully, respectfully.

When I heard Aunt Lizzy go over and say "Shut up" to June, I was elated. June was alive! I listened to Aunt Lizzy as she spoke to June's body through the sheer, white screen.

I wasn't yet aware that Butchy, Josh, Jr., and Little Tony were dead. No one told us. So I didn't know, as we fought for our lives, that we had missed their funeral. Mamma had missed it, too. The doctors had said that she would not be able to leave the hospital in her condition. Her heart was too weak and was fading fast.

Daddy, Ephraim, Dan, Esther and James, along with Lawrence, all went to their funeral and burial in a little town called Plattsburg. I heard later that it was a beautiful Homecoming, complete with praise and worship. It featured the local black preachers from Cameron, Saint Joseph, Leavenworth, KS., Kansas City, and, of course, Plattsburg. All of them gave glory to the Lord, as they comforted another black family that had become a victim of violence.

The police had ordered a decree not to allow the caskets open... But, truth be told, I battled with what the Lord was doing. The time at the hospital became a sort of "crossroads" for me. Pastor after pastor came in and prayed for us.

Over and over, I felt the Hand of God healing me... the very Hands that had been there to save my life.

And yet, at the same time, the evil spirits of anger and bitterness began to well up inside of me. I thought about that psychic that approached our home several years ago. She had said that our home was "wished in death." I understood now that we were cursed by someone, and not by God. I thought about Henry. I thought about Trixie. I thought about Jimmy and Billy and the KKK. I thought about how they were smiling, even laughing, as my body burned, as my brothers and nephew were burned alive.

Healing gave me time… too much time… time to think, time to put things together, time to grow increasingly ignited. Now I began to burn from the inside…

'Who had cursed us to begin with?' I wondered. Was it one of those always jealous, trifling black folks, always getting into someone's business, and then putting spells on you if they didn't like what you said? Or was it one of those evil, hating white folks, only thinking about how they could make another dollar? I knew that a "darky's life" wasn't worth ten cents compared to white profits. These were just smaller sample sizes of insistent control, repetitions of the lasting effects of colonization. How is it that they forced us over here, and then despised us for being here later? Strangely, I thought about Malcolm X and Martin Luther King. Then my thoughts hastened back to Henry.

Another possibility entered my mind… 'Or did we curse ourselves?' I wondered. 'Did all the fighting among ourselves open this door of evil?' I now had enough time to consider every angle…

Day after day, with the doctors and nurses amazed at our survival, Evelyn and I just kept living. One breath at a time… One heartbeat at a time...

Keep going… Keep breathing… Don't quit… Make it through the night, then let God help you again tomorrow…

But the inward struggle no one could see. The longer I thought, the more I was certain… The fire had been set on purpose. The pieces all came together. They couldn't get Daddy to relocate. The men came and put new paint on the house. The home went up in flames so quickly. That kind of fire wasn't natural. The paint had to be of some type of flammable substance! Someone might have saturated the shutters and new roof shingles with something that would burn. And the snowy ground burning? Snow doesn't burn! Even the metal fence continually flowed with fire across the outline of the yard. It was obvious to me that a flammable substance was the culprit.

The more I thought, the more my stomach clenched itself into knots of rage… Anger and bitterness welled up inside of me like a two-headed dragon.

I now knew, at least in my mind, that the fire had been set on purpose. The city administration wanted us out so badly for their new expansion. For a stupid golf course and swimming pool… they were willing to… to actually murder us! For the first time in my life, my innocence was replaced with complete wrath.

And then I thought about that man, the one staring at me in the doorway, watching my blood, my pain… And the more I thought, the more my two-headed dragon appeared. The only thing that kept me from exploding from within was my worry for my sister, June.

The white screen was still up between us. "June!" I would whisper loudly, repeatedly in the middle of the night. I either got a low moan or no answer at all. Then the pain in my body would flare up with such power I thought that I was going to pass on. But, in my misery, it was my thoughts about returning to my life with my loved ones that would sustain me. My hair was gone. My skin was gone, and I was too weak. Filled with pain, I was too scared to see what else was gone. Between fighting for my own life, Evelyn fighting for hers, and the reality that my two-headed dragon was becoming a bigger and bigger part of me, it was a wonder that I maintained my sanity.

I still wasn't out of the woods. I knew that Death wanted me. And more times than I care to admit, I wanted Death. Compared to this pain, Death seemed a warm, seductive ally. The grim Reaper became more and more a handsome and charming match for me. Me and Death, united in holy matrimony… until death do us part. Had I made a joke to myself? I don't know. I was going crazy.

Then the pain flared up… I screamed. The nurses brought in morphine. Sleep. Beautiful, magical, unconsciousness… Sleep.

I don't know how long I slept, but I awoke to see Daddy. Tears streamed down his face. I could tell that it killed him to look at me. I tried to speak, but nothing came out. I tried to open my eyes wider, but they wouldn't cooperate. But I could see Daddy clearly. I saw the anguish and fear from what he was looking at… looking at my condition. I must have looked horrid, my hair gone, my skin gone. Whiteness crept over my body like a foreign image, a silhouette of a kingly ghost.

My daddy leaned in and gently kissed me.

Daddy's arms were in bandages. He didn't say anything. He didn't need to. I read everything he was feeling… the regret from not moving… the way he was duped… the way he had failed to protect his family… I could tell that he placed all the blame on himself. Behind his eyes dwelt pure agony. My strong, heroic dad, who had always given us what we needed, now felt the total immersion of pure defeat. I read his eyes… "I failed."

I slept.

More days passed, but Daddy wouldn't leave our room. As the days went by, I would wake up and hear him talking to God. I heard the word 'help' and I heard the word 'vengeance'. At times, I would awaken to see his face in his hands, slumped over and just sobbing. Never had I seen my daddy so helpless.

I thought about all the black men who had felt this way in the land of their enemies… the unimaginable pain for black men through the ages, proud warriors and protectors, their children in chains and sold, their wives raped or taken as lovers against their will. How inconceivable the pain! And yet I witnessed it now right in front of me, a small, cruel sample of the 400-year pattern of a black man's agony, as it ate away at Daddy in that hospital room. Great leader Joshua, stubborn Joshua, victorious and resourceful Joshua... Yet, at least in his own eyes... had utterly fallen.

For some reason, this sight, this most horrible sight, made me break up with my flippant affair with Death. I wanted to live. For Daddy's sake, I needed to live.

I awoke one night to see Daddy sleeping in the chair next to my bed. A lamplight was on, and his bible rested on his lap.

"Daddy," I whispered. I hadn't been able to speak to him before. But now, my mouth was working fine again. "Daddy..."

He opened his eyes and looked into mine.

"It wasn't your fault, Daddy," I whispered as loud as I could.

His lower lip began to quiver. Then he looked down.

"I think they set the fire on purpose," I said.

"I know," he whispered back. "I know... but you need to get well. I don't know what I'll do if you..."

"I'm going to live, Daddy," I said strongly. "But I'm so angry, Daddy. They tried to... to... kill us. I want them to go to jail for the rest of their lives."

"Me, too," he muttered. I could see his frustration starting to surface. He looked back into my eyes. "But that's not important. What's important now is that you get better."

There was a long silence, as both of us momentarily went into our own thoughts.

"I can see the people's expressions when they look at me," I finally said. "I can see by the way they look at me... I must look terrible, Daddy."

Daddy leaned towards me. "Right now, you are the most beautiful woman I've ever seen."

Tears came into my eyes. "Daddy, I want them to get hurt, too, just like they hurt our family," I heard myself suddenly say.

Right then, as I verbalized my anger, I saw the mixed emotions on Daddy's face. I saw relief, because he knew I was going to be okay. He saw my spunk. And, if I had the tenacity for revenge, he knew that I had the strength to live. But then he gave me a puzzled look. Sitting back down in his chair he looked at the floor.

"I'm so happy you're gonna' live, Betty," he said. "You don't know how happy I am that I see you're gonna' live." It was good to see a passion of hope on Daddy's face again. "I want you to live so badly," he went on. "But I don't just want you to live... I... I... want you to... *LIVE*."

He looked over at me to see if I understood. I nodded, because I did.

"I didn't come see you and June 'til a few days ago, because I was so angry at them," he said. "And I was so ashamed... at me. First thing I did, after the funeral..."

"What funeral?" I interrupted.

Daddy stared at me for a moment and realized that I didn't know about the death of my two brothers and my nephew. "Your little brothers ... Junior and Butchy didn't make it," he said quietly. "And Little Tony died, too."

He looked at me, watching a tear emerge. "Everyone else made it?" I asked, ignoring the sting from the tears as they made their way down into my open wounds.

"Yes," he said. "Only you and June in here. Everyone else is okay."

"How's Mamma?"

"They got her back at the hospital." He hesitated. "But she's fine…"

I wasn't sure if he was telling the truth about Mamma being fine.

"First thing I did after the funeral…," he went on, restarting his story. "… was to go and get my gun. I was going to kill them all, starting with Jimmy and Billy…" He took a deep breath. "Besides my animals, my tools, and the garbage trucks, only two things I owned survived that fire… my gun and my bible. They were both out in the back shed."

Daddy mumbled on for a while about grabbing his gun and killing the men he thought started the fire.

"Daddy…" I wanted to stop him like I would have tried to stop Henry.

Daddy threw his hands up the way he does when he wants to say something, but inside doesn't know if he should say it or not..

"God stopped me," he said, shaking his head slowly. "Between the gun and the bible, I made the wrong choice. I just kept hearing, 'Twelve Hebrews, twelve Hebrews' over and over. I don't know what that meant, so I was compelled to go back to the shed to make the right exchange. And, when I turned to Hebrews twelve, I… I *hated* what it said… It said, 'Follow peace with all men, and holiness, without which no man shall see the Lord'. But that's the last thing I wanted to do, Betty!"

It seemed to me that lots of these people around this town never bothered to follow this scripture. *'Did they miss reading this?'* I thought to myself. I knew this because Daddy always talked about how many whites in town went to church, but how he never understood how their actions didn't line up with the holy scriptures.

"Betty…" he went on. "My wrath made me feel so… weak. 'Vengeance is mine,' said the Lord, 'I will repay.'"

"Wow," I whispered. I was so happy God had stepped in.

Daddy stopped, looked me over to see if he could touch any part of me that wasn't burnt, and then he found my left hand. "I'm telling you like He told me. There is a root of bitterness that comes that will defile you. It will steal your soul. It will make you act like them. And... and God told me... We ain't like them!"

He let go of my hand, clenched his fists, and set them on his knees. He took a deep breath. I could tell how much he was hurting, and that it would take some time to get over this.

"Bitterness took many of our People throughout history," he added. "It ain't fair, but bitterness took many of us away from our God."

He reached back and quickly squeezed my hand. "Hebrews said something else," he whispered. "It said that Esau was a profane man..." He looked at me with anger and sadness, and I wasn't sure which one was dominant. "Do you know what makes a profane man?" he asked, still squeezing.

"Dishonesty?" I threw out.

"Nah," he answered. "Jacob was more dishonest than Esau, truth be told... A profane man takes what is sacred and treats it like it ain't nothin'! He takes what God gave him and treats it like his own... like somethin' of little value!"

"What, Daddy?"

"We're always fallin' right into 'ol Satan's trap. "Always thinkin' 'bout our bellies... or... or getting' our entertainment... or our money... our... our... *stew.*" I quickly thought about Henry's letter that warned me about these same things. "That 'ol devil got a whole buffet for people that just want to eat for today... He always servin' up self-indulgence, self-pity, entitlement, hostility, pride... a side of revenge... and... and... then for dessert... *bitterness.* Then we become like... *THEM!*"

His last word shook the room. "Like them," he repeated more softly.

I saw how passionate he had become. I saw that he, too, had made a choice, like the crucified thieves, when he went back and chose his bible over his gun, peace over confusion, love over pain.

Maybe our crucified thieves' moments never stop coming and going all throughout our lives. I made a quick mental note to think more about that one later.

"Truth be told," he said sadly. "I should have stopped all that fussin' that was always goin' on in my home... I should have..."

"Daddy, you cannot take the blame. It didn't happen because of that! It happened, because of those..."

Daddy put his hand up for me to stop talking...

"God told me all this," he said. "I know where things started and ended..." He looked at me again with a strength that I know God put inside of him. Then he planted another kiss on my cheek. "And... and... I can only do what is my part to do," he finished. "I can only control my own actions!"

Before my very eyes, the old Joshua, the hero, had risen up again... thanks to God. He spoke with determination again. While watching us get healed, he had been healed. While watching us fight for our lives, he had been fighting for his. And now he spoke with the demeanor of a superhero. My superhero...

"I have loved righteousness and hated wickedness," he quoted. "And they are selling their inheritance in heaven for a... a... a damn golf course!"

He looked up at me with conviction.

"We are being held for a different place, Betty... Mount Sion... The whole bible is written, telling us how we're different and how we belong to Him... and how our destiny will be the opposite of theirs... if...if... *if we overcome and keep His commandments. Our Lord went through far more than us!"*

I began to cry. My heart was healing as I felt my two-headed dragon start to dissipate. I sobbed away the monster in my stomach. It left as my body rejoiced. My anger fled at that very moment.

Daddy recognized God's touch and was happy. "But I'm still praying every day for God's vengeance. That's what I'm now praying for every hour of every day! I know He don't want me to do it, but I'm praying it gets done. Our greatest victory as fighters sometimes is just to get outta' His way!"

"That's some good preachin'," I said weakly with a smile. It reminded me of Henry's.

"I'm gonna' go see your mamma now," he said, getting up to leave.

"Daddy," I whispered. I wasn't sure how to tell him everything I was feeling. I was overwhelmed with grief, pain, and confusion, all at once. "Josh, Butchy... and... and Little Tony... Do you..." I began to cry again. "Do you think they suffered much?"

"I think we live in a cruel world," Daddy answered slowly. "But I think God was with them, and I think He took them quickly." He lifted a hand to the heavens.

Daddy took one last look at me before moving towards the door. I saw the anguish on his face, but the love that I saw in his eyes was pure.

"It sounds real strange, I know, Betty," he stopped and said.

I saw the quick wince, followed by his fist hitting his chest. He tried to hide his vulnerability. He turned. Now facing the wall, he said, "But God stirs up a black man so that he finally has pride... And then he asks him to renounce that same pride later." He looked back at me and smiled. "But that's the healthy order of things for us black folk... least ways for black men."

Then he went around the screen and prayed for June, who was still unconscious.

"Is June okay, Daddy?"

"Yeah," I heard him say. "She's gonna' make it fine, just like you, Betty." I was so happy, again, to receive confirmation that June was still alive. I know June heard him, too, and what a difference his words made to our hearts compared to the words of those from the doctor.

"I love you, June," I yelled over to her.

After kissing June on the forehead, Daddy came back around. "She still not awake…"

He looked at me, not wanting to leave me.

Then he bent over to give me one last kiss before leaving. With his cheek glued next to mine, I heard him whisper, "The first shall be last, and the last first." He stood up straight and lifted his head with dignity. "God told me that He ain't gonna' turn the order of people upside-down…" He beamed at me to make sure I was listening. "He said He gonna' turn them back right-side up! People been different since the Esau and Jacob division. It was me that should've been teachin' y'all 'bout us bein' Hebrews… not Henry." I saw guilt reciprocating on his face. "I was afraid," he went on. "But then I realized, it's what you *don't* know that ends up hurtin' you a whole lot more. We're Judah, and that's what the world doesn't want us to…"

His voice trailed off.

He was tired.

"I only know two things," he ended. "Justice always comes, and…" He stopped. "Git yo' rest, Betty."

He picked up his bible to leave. He smiled and started again for the door with a slight limp.

218

"Daddy," I stopped him before he closed the door. I wanted to know everything the Lord had told him. His words were such a powerful remedy. "You said that you know two things," I said. "What's the second thing?"

He looked at me carefully before answering.

"The other thing I know for sure…"

He closed his eyes... and tapped himself on the chest again. "Is that…"

"…*We ain't like them*," he whispered emphatically, before walking out.

16

"When the Good Come Out of Hiding"

During my long stay in that cold hospital bed, I went from having a revival to having a relapse. My lungs.

And now, not only did the stinging burns torment me day and night, but it had also become difficult to breathe. My swollen air passages threatened to shut down continually. I was now having delusions. I wasn't sure if this part was real, or part of a dream. But, in my visions, the doctors walked out of my room into the hallway. Once there, they took off masks that I didn't know they were wearing. Underneath, there were the faces of destruction. They laughed. Then they saw more of my family members, coming towards my room. They hissed and spit and cussed, put their faces back on, smiled, and then courteously said, "Hello."

'What was that?' I asked myself. The visions frightened me.

The Church, sensing I needed help and hearing about the relapse, began returning to the hospital again.

Into the room came Elder Davis, the partially blind pastor of the Pentecostal Church in Plattsburg, the place where June and I often hung out on weekends. The pastor had just come from a Sunday service preaching over in Leavenworth, Kansas, when the Spirit told him to leave the Christmas dinner and come over to the hospital in

Cameron. The young man that drove him had gotten lost. So Elder Davis undertook the painstaking efforts to lead him to the hospital.

"A blind man had to show you the way to get here," Elder Davis fussed jokingly, as they entered the room.

The young man looked a little embarrassed. Then, after guiding Elder Davis's hand as to where he should pray for me, he couldn't control the horrified expression any longer. It was as if he'd seen a monster. I was glad that Elder Davis was blind.

"Thank you," he softly told the young man.

"Her hair…" I heard the young man say.

Earlier that day, I had asked someone to hold up a mirror. I had to face what I was going to see. I was shocked and sickened by my bald, burned scalp. I began to sob. "I lost all my hair…"

I was slightly astonished at the level of concerned vanity that I still held. After all, this wasn't my fault. Still I had a tinch of blaming myself or at least my skin color. Why? I wasn't sure.

"You will have hair again," Elder Davis articulated with confidence. "I have no doubt that you…"

Then he began to speak in an unknown language. I had been around church long enough to recognize real tongues from false ones. This one smoothly reverberated with beauty and clarity. I could tell it was, not only real communication with the God of the universe, but it was accompanied with prophesy and accuracy. He understood what I felt. God's Love. I felt God's Power.

"You will have hair," he whispered for the second time. "You will have healing. Your air waves are opening. You will impact many people and guide them to God's Kingdom. You will not only live, but you will live with purpose and influence."

Needless to say, my hair grew back more fully than ever!

But It was there… right there in that hospital room, that I saw the war play out… the battle for our bodies, our minds, and our very souls. I became adept at seeing all the combatants "play out their hand" on every level. I saw the true powers of both sides of the spirit world, as they both engaged in a "tug-o-war" with my life and my soul.

Which side would win?

June and I had the real Church people, as I mentioned. These people oozed with real love and victory! When they left, I was lifted beyond description. Then you had the fake church people, with no other agenda than to satisfy their personal senses of obligation or console their consciences… These people were as effective as a dog wandering into the wrong house. They did nothing measurable. I would just watch them "sniff around" awkwardly, mutter a few memorized, meaningless prayers, and then finally mosey back towards the door.

"Hope you and your sister feel better soon!" they would wave, shaking their heads, as I watched them disappear around the nurses' station. They had a clear agenda. They took hidden jabs at you. These were disguised as "caretakers", God seekers, like spiritual hitmen. The enemies of the world, undercover racists or greedy businessmen, would come to satisfy a curiosity for themselves about my condition, and deliver a report as to whether evil had defeated us.

Anyone and everyone came into our room for a variety of motives. It was amazing to me to see how many of the town's citizens were regular churchgoers, and even held positions within their religious organizations.

I recall Henry once telling me, "A lot of church folks aren't going to make it. The bible tells us to be Jesus folks, not church folks, and to love, not go to church again and again… It's not a Sunday thing. It's a 7-days-a-week thing…"

Then you had the newspaper reporters and television crews. They did all they could to convince the nurses and security that they were all there for us, but they were quickly shooed away. Still, our story ended up on television anyway, as well as in newspapers and magazines. We received so many cards from all over everywhere! Black, white, and various peoples from all over the world wrote us!

Why so many were interested in our story and how they heard our story, I'm still not sure. But the sadistic tug-o-war waged on.

It seemed like this war had similarities with the same one our ancestors confronted every day of their enslaved lives… to live or to die… to survive or concede to the relentless pain… My life had been reduced to trying to survive a few more minutes with Agony as my only companion. However, I was cast into this nightmarish predicament for only a few months. I couldn't imagine how our ancestors had lived out this crisis every day of their earthly existence.

But, it seemed, I still had a say… One side was going to win. My body appealed to the choice of my mind, while my mind looked inquisitively towards my faith. Yeshua, like Henry called Him, He who held the keys, seemed to have left the choice to me.

Death waited at the door for an answer. The Spirit of Life also waited.

Night was the worst time. In the darkness, I sometimes awoke gasping for breath. My heart would pound wildly as the pain from my burns welled up again. I would dream of the black smoke from the trains as I walked resolutely into my death. But suddenly I would come out on the other side, and I would see the same vision I had after George's death… slaves working in the fields… And then one slave in particular would notice me. He stood straight up and noticed me looking. The slave's gaze, filled with emptiness, penetrated mine. He seemed to ask, "What are you doing here?" Then a distant voice of another worker would sing a spiritual… "And when I come to die, give me peaceful grace ..." the melody echoed through the fields...

Then and there, on that hospital bed, I continually examined my very own soul. Where I found my life hanging in the balance, I decided to live differently... if I made it.

I had been baptized, because "it was the right thing to do". I was told that it was possible to go down a dry devil and come up a wet one... Had I used it to feed my assurance, and the church used me to support livelihoods and clubs? Were these nothing more than worldly ambitions with His Name falsely attached?

Instead of using His grace to live for Him, I came to the realization that I had used my salvation to feel better and entertain myself. My Jesus life had become like a sick person taking drugs... "Pop two scriptures and call Me in the morning." As Henry had warned, maybe my salvation had become a facade of religious obligation, while my life bore no resemblance to Him.

Had my road to heaven become a self-absorbed path to self-medication and justification? Had the gifts He gave me been used like trivial side shows, like circus acts?

Was I being deceived? Was I living deceived?

I remember Henry reading from the Holy scriptures... "This people honors Me with their lips, but their hearts are far from Me," Jesus had warned. "In vain do they worship Me, teaching for doctrines the commandments of men. You reject the commandment of God that you may keep your own tradition."

Had God's true commands been exchanged for watered-down, man-made traditions?

Tradition, tradition, TRADITION!!! My brain couldn't extinguish the pressure from this sudden examination or even decipher which conclusion was true.

As I fought for my life, a miracle happened that I never would have guessed would happen in a million years. A new flow of goodness, like cool water on a scalding-hot day, had emerged from the least-suspecting source.

The town of Cameron came out of hiding.

It seemed that everyone had been touched, on some level, by that fatal fire. The active folks always silence those who hide. But now...

People... white people... specifically, our hometown people, some of whom I didn't know, came forth and helped our family.

A man named Petty Brown, who owned a big, two-story home, told us that we could all stay at his house until we had another place to stay. And we did. Daddy, Ephraim, Lawrence, Esther, and James... all moved in with Mr. Brown and his wife. They were given nice beds, softer than they had ever known. Meals were prepared for them four times a day. People brought over donated clothes. New clothes and other items, hundreds of dollars of donations, were even laid at the Brown's door.

Silver's Theater in downtown Cameron arranged and sponsored a show to raise money on our behalf. The show was titled, "Somebody Up Here Loves You." Nearly everyone showed up, and all the proceeds were contributed to our family.

When evil would try to respond, it seemed the good white folks came in droves to run them away. The paint company sent Daddy a notice that he had to pay for the paint that had helped ignite the burning of our home! An attorney stepped in named Mr. Clever. He represented Daddy for free. And even though the painting company threatened a lawsuit, Mr. Clever was prepared to meet them in court. "Lives were lost," Mr. Clever told them. "These people are all paid up and that is the end of that."

Daddy never heard from the paint company again. But that wasn't enough for Mr. Clever. He then escorted Daddy to the hospital, and Mamma was taken out and brought home again. Mr. Clever was letting everyone in the community know, even the KKK and the police, that we were not to be messed with.

As Daddy's trash trucks ran their routes, people would come out to give donations and gifts... everything from shoes to fresh-baked pies to bottles of whiskey. A separate pick-up truck was contributed to help gather the items. They were then taken and unloaded for them at the Brown's.

The Cameron people sponsored everything from lemonade stands to garage sales in order to raise money for our family. And, when it was all said and done, the town had bought us a house on Orange Street, and Daddy was able to buy three acres of land behind it! 'Wasn't this great! Some white people really care!' I thought. These kind, loving acts by the Cameron citizens changed my feelings forever...

It was so strange and miraculous... What could change hearts so quickly? Was this the prayers of the saints? Or maybe this was where the city wanted us to live all along! Were people moved to actions that actually mattered, like the Good Samaritan... where crucified thieves confessed the permanent destinies of their hearts?

I was humbled.

I now felt I had so much to learn. When good people finally move, there is power! I was overwhelmed as I floated on this plateau, watching and hearing of God's People as they acted out their silent faith. It was here, among these good deeds, that I rested on God's resources, getting strengthened before proceeding higher up the mountain of knowledge...

I realized then, the greatest healing was not the return of my hair or even my temporal life... It was the possession of a new heart... a heart that could actually love folks... a heart that could actually forgive those who did me harm.

People came forward, one by one, two by two... testifying to authorities, to newspapers, to anyone that would hear... that the fire had been set on purpose!

As I remained in the hospital, a man came to speak to Mamma and Daddy, who were sitting on the back porch of Mister Brown's house. He sat down and looked at them both.

"I'm so sorry about your loss," he said softly.

"Thank you," Mamma replied.

The man fumbled with a set of keys in his hands. He seemed nervous. He looked over his left, then his right shoulder, then glanced up at the back windows. He was seeing if anyone else was listening. Satisfied that no one else was around, he suddenly blurted out, "It was set."

"What?" Daddy asked.

The man fidgeted slightly with his keys, looking down. "The fire," he whispered softly, still looking down. "It was set."

"The fire was set on purpose?" Mamma pressed him on to speak.

"Yes, ma'am," he answered, finally looking back into their eyes.

"How do you know?" Daddy asked. Although he knew, he wanted details... from a white witness. "Who did it?"

"Well, it was just set," the man repeated.

And that was all he said before quickly departing. Who this man was or how he knew, we never did find out. Yet he came out of his comfort zone to let us know.

A few months later several townsfolk walked into the police station and filed reports on what they knew or what they heard. I suspect that they knew, deep inside, that it probably wouldn't do much good... After all, the written testimonies were going right into the hands of Jimmy and Billy, the leaders and instigators of the "good 'ol boys" club of hatred.

But they did it anyway...

Nothing was ever done, and no one was ever brought to justice. Jimmy and Billy danced around the outside investigators and reporters who had suddenly appeared in town.

Sometimes they performed tactfully with real professional skills. Other times, they were their usual selves, brutish and impatient. They came out with their own investigation, of course, stating that the fire started with our own negligence from 'not maintaining a good and healthy fireplace'. They stated in their paperwork that the old wood-burning stove was also too old for use. But the fire on the snow, and the nearly instantaneous combustion of the complete home... None of this did the sheriff's office address in their reports.

The witness statements were filed under "not proven" and stuffed away. Now you know this was the same kinda' thing those two town officers did with Uncle Joshua. "Timber fell on his head." That was all that was said and nothing more.

But there was a definite sense of justice that coaxed our pain like a medicine... to actually hear white men and women gossiping that a black family, our family, had been attacked and coerced for the simple reason to relocate a golf course along with a new swimming pool.

A few magazines and newspapers ran the story about the night of the fire and included a thorough background of past patterns of racism, inequality, and even murder in the areas of Northwest Missouri. The hanging of the young black man in St. Joseph was included.

Ultimately, nothing was ever officially done, of course. I suspect that, in a perfect world, murder charges and arrests would have helped with our closure and pain. But, in our world, and in those times, white men and women telling the truth against their own was so taboo... Well, let's just say the testimonies that we got were enough to be appreciated beyond words.

And it was more than we could have hoped for.

I can never fully determine what is inside of a man or woman's heart. Some may boldly go out on a limb for righteousness in order to clear their own conscience... It might have been that, that was the only way those people could sleep at night or live with themselves. They had to come forward. They had to push for justice. They had a fear of God. And their selfish lack of empathy somehow persistently, inwardly tormented them like a splinter in their hearts. Hearts to be poked at, convicted, until the splinter falls out, leaving nothing but a bloody vacancy.

No matter the cost now, some knew they would meet God one day, and would have to provide answers for their silence.

But there's another kind of man... the kind that can go to his grave secretly knowing the most awful things imaginable. He sleeps fine at night, especially after indulging in some written-out prescriptions mixed with homemade remedies and alcoholic beverages... He further dulls his already dull cares for anyone outside of himself. He lives out his days in fine fashion. He has no sense of guilt. Indeed, he has no heart at all, it seems. This man has no "ears to hear or eyes to see", because his ears are mounted on backwards to listen only to his own thoughts, and his eyes are constantly trained to see only his own sense of well-being.

He literally can't see you... let alone feel with you. He only knows how to use you... for his own gain, for his own glory... or maybe just to keep you oppressed as a means of deflecting the spotlight from his own blemishes and weaknesses. His pride and gluttony always keeps himself from any form of genuine self-reflection.

And he is willing to die that way. Pride is a powerful evil. Then there's yet another kind of man...

This man is a victim of his own birthright... and doesn't have the heart to bear it, nor the tools to change it.

A young man like this was only 10-years-old, named Johnny Shadows, Jr., who was devastated after hearing about the fire. He had been the best friend of Butchy, my brother who had been killed. His father, Mr. Shadows, was the town's store owner. His father also happened to be the Imperial Wizard of the local KKK.

One day after school, Johnny confronted his dad. "Why, Dad?" he cried out, as he rushed into the store. He was now exhausted from the hurt. Weekends he had spent in the woods crying. And during the week? He was desperately trying to focus in school and survive in a home of cold affluence and seething hatred. But now he just couldn't fake any longer. Johnny only had one friend who he could talk with... Butchy, the only one who sat with him at lunch, who laughed at his jokes, who understood him...

Now his days were filled with loss, and the thoughts of his best friend being burned alive haunted him all night. In his mind, he heard his screams... he saw his friend reaching for help... he witnessed his own version of the flames overcoming Butchy over and over and over again...

And he couldn't stop the thoughts. They relentlessly consumed him. The thoughts were so excruciating that, at times, he himself couldn't breathe. He, himself, felt the heat and digested the smoke he imagined smothering Butchy. Fear pounded at his out-of-control heart. He was losing his mind, as evil spirits delighted in another assignment from a father's curse.

"Why did he have to die?" he screamed at his dad, who was busy with a customer. This day, Johnny didn't care. He had to know. He had to confront his father. "It's bad enough that you hate them. Why did you have to kill them?"

Another store clerk, in the form of an overweight, middle-aged woman caught the eyes of Mr. Shadows, who quickly looked around for help... and for possible witnesses. She did a quick nod at him and took over for him in helping the customer he had been assisting.

Mr. Shadows' face turned red as he grabbed Johnny's arm and took him swiftly into the back of the store.

"Don't you ever question me in front of my customers!" he whispered threateningly with a finger pointing right in the face of his son.

"But why?" Johnny kept yelling, staring into his father's eyes. "Why did y'all have to..."

Just then, Mr. Shadows flat-handedly smacked his son flush across his face.

"What did I tell you 'bout hangin' out with them niggers?" he went on. He momentarily peeked outside the door to see if anyone was listening.

Johnny looked down. He was scared. He was hurt. He was ashamed of who he was. Then he lifted his head boldly, looking right at his father. "He was my friend," Johnny said.

He slapped Johnny again...

A small trickle of blood crept out of Johnny's nostril. He looked up at his dad again. Refusing to give up he continued...

"But... he... was... my friend!"

Mr. Shadows started to slap Johnny a third time. But he held up his last blow, as he saw his son's determination and willingness to take another hit for Butchy.

"We are family!" his dad whispered loudly. "We are blood!"

"I hate you," Johnny screamed. "I don't want to be your blood!"

A third slap quickly followed.

Johnny tore himself away from his father's grip and ran out the back door of the store.

At the hospital, as I started to succumb to another night of sweet sleep on my miracle bed... or deathbed... It was yet to be decided. But my mind took me to a clear recollection of another cold night at the tracks. I was talking to Henry in front of the fire, with Trixie listening intently. "When will all this evil end?"

"When He comes back," Henry had reflected somberly. "Or..." He glanced up at me doubtfully. "... when the good come out of hiding... whichever comes first. We can get many small victories over evil when the good folks come out of hiding..."

Just then, I heard the door open to my hospital room... back to reality, back to pain. I was wide awake to see who it was. Somebody just stood in the shadow of my doorway.

I waited...

Slowly, walking into the dim light that shined from above my bed, emerged a woman. She had greasy, reddish-blond hair that framed her face from premature wrinkles caused by a stress-filled life.

'Where did I know this woman from?' I wondered. 'What does she want?'

Then, slowly, her features formed into the recognition of someone I knew long ago... "Suzy?" I gasped.

It was Suzy! She looked so old. She looked so sad... Then tears began to flow down her cheeks.

Trying to talk, she wanted to say my name, but all I could hear was, "B... B... Be... Bet..." Her mouth quivered, and she couldn't speak.

She quit trying. She fell to her knees, put her forehead against the side of my bed... and wept. I could only hear the uncontrollable, violent sobs as they gushed out.

Within several minutes, she poured out her penitence... Drowning in sorrow, she continued to weep.

Suzy, the advocate for the smaller, the defender against the bullies... on the baseball field. The lines on her face had made themselves one with the dimensions of time... slowly, yet surely, coming for their debt, a glory to be paid.

She finally finished her crying and wiped her eyes. She didn't have to speak. I saw what she had come to confess.

Her eyes sparkled, she smiled. Within those few moments, Suzy looked at least twenty years younger... a thousand-pound, invisible burden had been lifted.

Without a word, she turned and exited, walking lightly in her new-found freedom...

Meanwhile, after work, Mr. Shadows drove up to his beautiful home on the outskirts of town. The Shadows' house represented one of the town's lovely "mansions", surrounded by a regal wrought iron gate and perfect landscaping that resembled a stony, museum-like structure. It sat proudly in the dark, quaintly lit by two fancy lamp posts that highlighted the huge front door.

Mr. Shadows was angry. He was looking for Johnny.

He walked past his wife, who was waiting to greet him. She handed him a glass of whiskey that she had poured just minutes before his arrival. .

"Where is that spoiled-rotten, nigger-loving brat of yours?" he asked, ignoring his wife's welcome. He quickly guzzled down the drink.

His frustrations towards Johnny weren't new.

"I saw him go to his room," Mrs. Shadows said. She set the bottle of whiskey down and flopped herself back onto the sofa in front of the television.

She heard her husband's footsteps pound up the stairs before coming back down again.

"Not up there," he blurted out.

He walked outside to the back yard, cursing to himself. After a few minutes, he came back into the room, angrier than ever.

"Do you know what that little, ungrateful son-of-a-bitch did today?" he asked.

Mrs. Shadows' eyes were glued to the television, as she plopped a chocolate-covered strawberry into her mouth. She was fully engaged in an episode of "Father Knows Best", one of her favorite TV shows on CBS.

"He embarrassed me, Margaret," he continued his uproar, not bothering to wait for a reply. "That little bastard came into my store and embarrassed me in front of several customers!"

Mrs. Shadows chuckled. Her eyes were still glued to the television.

"Margaret!" he yelled.

She stopped watching television and turned towards him.

"Well, honey, he's going through a hard time," she defended her son while glancing back at the television. "You know that one of those boys who died in the fire was his best friend…"

"I know that nigger was his best…"

Mitch Shadows, now fully belligerent, picked up what was left from the bottle of whiskey and gulped it down to the last drop. Then he hurled the bottle against the wall. He now had his wife's full attention.

"Now look at what you did!" he exclaimed. "Now you have more crap to clean up…"

She stared submissively… a defeated, wounded shell of the joyous, single woman she had been.

"This is important, Margaret!!" he continued to bark.

She jumped up from the couch and began picking up the pieces of glass. "He's reaching out to you, Mitch," she said, briefly looking up. "You're going to mess up our new carpet, you big lug…"

Feeling disgusted with her reply, he went out the backdoor again, grumbling while slamming the door behind him.

"Johnny!" he yelled into the night air. "Get the hell in here, you bastard! I know you hear me!" He looked past the swimming pool, past the garden, past the basketball court, and into the woods behind their home. "Boy, you're gonna' get it when I find you!"

Mr. Shadows marched back into the house. His anger was now directed back towards his wife. But Mrs. Shadows was used to these ordeals… the fights, the arguments, story after story, night after night, about the colored folks in town… about the one that Johnny hung out with… She had already anticipated this repeat performance, especially tonight having heard that Johnny's best friend had died.

She threw a handful of glass into the kitchen trash.

"We've given that boy everything," he went on muttering. "And this is how he repays us?"

"Check the basement," she suggested, before he could say anything more. "Sometimes he goes down there when he's upset."

Mr. Shadows, hands on his hips, hesitated for an instant, before heading for the basement door.

"Johnny!" he yelled down the stairs.

No answer. Mitch Shadows saw a light on, and he could smell alcohol.

"You bastard," he muttered as he marched down the stairs. "You've been in my whiskey again, you little son-of-a-..."

There was now a disturbing silence.

After several minutes, Mrs. Shadows walked to the basement door to peer down the stairs.

"Are you okay down there, Mitch?" she yelled.

Faintly, ever so softly, she heard weeping...

"Mitch?" she yelled. "Mitch... are you down there?"

No answer. Then she heard it again... distant whimpering, a sniffle, and then more whimpering.

She ran down the stairs to find her husband on his knees. He was holding a letter and crying. She quietly tiptoed closer in order to read what had upset her husband. She had never seen him cry before. Even after accidentally shooting their only other child, Johnny's older brother, Kyle, in a hunting accident, she had never seen him cry... not even at the funeral...

"I went to be with Butchy." the letter read.

Then she saw her son's favorite black and white *Converse* sneakers. But they were strangely suspended in midair. She looked up to see the rest of him, his neck attached to a rope that had been wrapped over a beam.

Mrs. Shadows let out a cry that could be heard all over Cameron that night...

I imagine it sounded a lot like the scream from Pharaoh's wife in Egypt the night of our deliverance, the night God executed their firstborn.

Joshua Jackson, in his most angry, hurting moments, had prayerfully relinquished any form of revenge by his own hand. He had turned all vengeance over to God.

And this was not good news for the guilty... It seemed now that vengeance had begun...

17

"After You Attend Your Own Funeral"

It was a beautiful sunny day in March of 1959 when Evelyn June and I came out of the hospital together. We insisted that we walk out, although the hospital had provided us with wheelchairs for the occasion. The hospital personnel knew that they were on display. But so did we. We wanted to do it our way. A small crowd was gathered outside to greet us, including photographers, newspaper reporters, and even television news crews.

Daddy, Ephraim, Dan, and Lawrence walked out with us. It felt so strange to be on my feet again. I ignored the pain of my pulling scar tissue and focused on walking without falling.

"How does it feel to be out of the hospital?" a reporter asked, sticking a microphone close to my face.

June, ever the talkative one, uncharacteristically remained silent. She looked at me, as did everyone else.

"It feels like we're born again," I said softly with a smile.

The crowd erupted with laughter! Questions came at us all at once. Daddy took my arm.

"We're going to get them home," he said to the crowd, moving us towards his pickup truck. "We have a home-cooked meal waiting for them…"

He lifted both of us, ever so gently, into the front seat, while Ephraim, Dan, and Lawrence jumped into the back.

The reporters seemed to want more. I rolled down the window of the truck to appease them. "We want to thank everyone who visited us and helped our family," I said loudly to them. The truck pulled away. "... and for all the prayers!" I yelled back with a wave.

"Aren't you the press correspondent?" Ephraim yelled from the back of the pickup, as we started towards home.

"Yeah, Mrs. David Brinkley!" Dan chimed in.

We all laughed. It was so nice to laugh again, and even nicer to be outside.

Tragedies happened so swiftly in black homes... Healings had to be even swifter or the bitterness would eat you alive. We could choose to live with anger, or we could choose to live with triumph... either way, I cried with tears of joy that God spared me from the grave.

However, life goes on...

They say that tragedy and near-death experiences can bring a closeness to God. I now knew that this was true because of my dual strategy to mentally and physically survive. You either learn to rely on God every day, or you succumb to what this pitiful world has to offer... which ain't much.

Would you believe me if I told you that the horrible fire brought such blessings? I now understood a mystery that only a small minority could relate to. One of those was a man named Joseph in the bible. His brothers sold him as a slave. They had removed him from his home and the love of a father. They had destroyed everything that he had known, moved him to a strange land, and then he was placed in confinement for a crime that he didn't commit.

Sounds exactly like our story... the true tragedy of the African Americans thrown into America...

But I like what Joseph said when he came out on the other side as Pharaoh's right-hand man. The day he met those conniving, guilty brothers, he said to them, "But as for you, you meant evil against me; but God meant it for good, in order to bring it about as it is this day, to save many people alive."

Joseph kept his eye on the big picture.

He didn't lose himself.

He didn't lose his God.

He didn't lose his purpose...

Now it was my turn.

After all, this is still real life. God is still God. Yeshua still hasn't come back. And I am still a black Hebrew, who could be used to "save many people alive"!

I began to consider myself a further extension of His higher purpose... God could use me... God could use you, too....

And so we lived on. Healing was not instantaneous. I could see the childlike innocence that June had lost. I often caught her frowning and having an unusually low countenance. And that just wasn't like the June Bug that I had known.

All of us had changed in our own way. Some time after the fire, Esther and her husband divorced, perhaps being unable to handle the repercussions from the fateful night that took a piece of us all. Esther went from having a husband, a lover, and a new child... to being alone now. I found her often crying out to God in a private bedroom, before walking stoically back in to join us in the dining room where we often played cards. I was proud of how she carried on. I was amazed how God picked her up, day after day...

Mamma began to go to church a lot more. It didn't matter if anyone went with her. She faithfully arose Sunday mornings, and dutifully grabbed her bible after Wednesday supper, and walked out the door to meet with her Lord. In her own way she seemed to have drawn closer to Him than before... At times, one of us would find our bible and trot after to join her. Sometimes we didn't. Either way, if she left a bit gloomy, she came home with a smile. Church became her therapy.

One Wednesday evening, I caught Daddy primping in the mirror after dinner. He had on his best overalls and cologne. As Mamma finished the dishes, folded her apron, and snatched up her bible, Daddy followed her out the door. He caught her about a half-block up the street. Without a word, he put his hand into hers and walked beside her...

The sun went down. The church bell rang. The choir could be heard starting their joyful chorus...

As Mamma and Daddy approached, both stared straight ahead... both smiled...

It was now about six months after the fire. After watching Mamma and Daddy heading to God's House on a Wednesday summer evening, I realized another truth.

No one, meaning none of our people, are protected from discrimination. It still rips through our society, like a lightning strike flashing over the atmosphere, over the oceans, over the whole earth.

All of us died in some way that fateful night. All of us turned to God. All of us, in our own way, went to our own funerals.

Therefore, the evil, the anger, life's depression... was unable to latch on to any of us. None of us turned to crime or activities of self-destruction such as drinking, gambling, or drug use. In a world where many people would justify unrighteous behaviors due to tragic events, we never did.

Sometimes, the depression of an oppressed people will come out in other ways such as arguing, fighting, blaming one another, killing... While we should be seeking many avenues meant to revive the soul, some will actually end up destroying it. We stuck with God. United with our first love. We lived His doctrine to follow peace with all men. We waited for His vengeance. If any revenge or reaping was going to come to those who did wrong, it was going to have to be God that would bring it.

Weeks turned into months. Months turned into years. And, while on full display to a host of Northwest Missouri witnesses, none of us grew to hate a race of man, as far as I knew. None of our family wallowed in bitterness or self-pity. None of us even moved out of Missouri! However, that was not the case with everyone else...

In 1968, on one of those hot, still, Missouri summer nights, the kind where you have to focus to breathe, Jimmy took a stroll out on the brand-new golf course. The moonlight shined brilliantly off of the green, well-maintained grass. He was alone. He had been drinking heavily. For whatever reason, Jimmy took out his pistol... the same pistol he had used so often to intimidate as many black folks as possible.

He was now haunted by the few black patrons still under his authority. But he forced himself to focus on, what he now viewed, as the inevitable task at hand...

Then he shot himself in the head.

Daddy insisted that we attend Jimmy's funeral. Only Mamma had the authority to tell him no, so she stayed home.

The strange thing is, our family made up about half the people who attended his memorial services at the local funeral home... Because of Jimmy's sister, Marge Shadows, the ex-mother of the now-dead son who loved my brother Butchy, and despite her now ex-husband's status in the KKK, we were graciously welcomed into Jimmy's service.

None of our family members said anything, as we walked into the funeral home and sat down.

Even when the town's Mayor Billings said that Jimmy was an honorable and just police officer, we all remained silent...

What an abnormal service it was! No one other than Jimmy's sister was there from his family, not even his ex-wife. It suddenly dawned on me that Jimmy didn't have much of a real family. Five members of the local KKK filled the front row in full Klan attire. They kept turning around to frown at us... They wore their shiny, white robes, but they kept their hoods and hats off. The high-ranking Mitch Shadows sat among them, giving awkward glances towards his ex-wife, Margaret... and us. The mayor and Billy sat together in the second row. A couple of other men, local law enforcement officers, sat in the third row. Our family filled up the entire back row.

The owner of the funeral parlor, taking on the role of the speaker, opened a bible, and began to read in front of Jimmy's closed casket...

"Ecclesiastes three..." he began, pausing briefly. "To everything there is a season, ... and a time to every purpose under the heaven. A time to be born, and a time to die; a time to plant, and a time to pluck up that which is planted." He closed the bible and started to speak.

But, to everyone's shock, Daddy stood up and cleared his throat. "A time to kill," he said, before the parlor owner went on. "And a time to heal. A time to break down, and a time to build up... verse three."

The men in the first three rows turned around to look at Daddy, but Daddy looked steadily   at the casket. The Klansmen gave intimidating, hate-filled scowls. I swallowed hard. Oh, how I wished I were somewhere else at that moment. 'Please God, don't let nothing happen', I softly spoke to myself.

But it only got worse...

One member of the Klan stood up and faced us. '*Oh, Lord,*' I thought. 'Here we go....'

"A time to keep silence," the man clenched his fist before pointing a finger at Daddy. "And a time to speak... Verse *seven!*"

'*He clearly knows his bible,*' I thought. I was impressed.

Another Klansman stood up beside him and simply shouted, "Yeah!"

I was thinking about God's timing. My head was down. I didn't want to look up. I said a quick, silent prayer.

And then I realized what Daddy was doing.

The sly Joshua, always a step ahead of his enemies and outsmarting them. He wasn't going to have this clash play out in the dark woods. No, he was going to settle this in the light, in front of witnesses, in front of the mayor, the police, and even the Klan...

"A time to love, and a time to hate," Daddy said calmly, still looking at the casket. "A time of war, and a time of..." He now looked right into the eyes of the Klansman. "... peace."

The Klansman gave an evil grin. "Wasn't much of a war, boy."

Daddy nodded towards the casket. "For him it was."

The funeral parlor, wanting to end the ceremony, quickly jumped in and said, "So help me, God... Thank you all for attending and don't forget to sign the book in back." He quickly walked out.

"Nope," the mayor stood up and said. "There's one more order of business that I would like to address." He cleared his throat and smiled. "I figure this is as good of time as any," the mayor went on. "Billy, come on up here, son!"

Billy stood up and walked to the front. He stood beside the mayor. He seemed uncomfortable, as he fidgeted while grasping the gun in his holster. He briefly glanced our way to let us know he was uncomfortable with us there. As inappropriate as it seemed, Billy wore his regular police uniform, and even kept his hat on. He even continued to gnaw on his wad of chew.

"Son, we're counting on you now," the mayor said. He took a shiny, new sheriff's badge out of a small box and its wrapper. He pinned it on Billy. "Congratulations, son. You've earned it!"

Everyone seemed to wait for Billy to say something, but Billy had nothing to say. He awkwardly shook the hand of the mayor and went to sit down. The mayor and the Klansmen all began to clap loudly. Those sitting, except for us, all rose to their feet. They looked at Billy and then back at us.

Then Daddy stood up. *'Oh, no, Lord'*, I thought. 'Please, please, *please…*'

All eyes turned to Daddy. But, to everyone's surprise, Daddy simply began to clap for Billy. One by one, we all took his cue, as we stood to our feet joining the applause. The Klan stopped clapping at that point. They just stood there with their mouths slightly open. All of them had a confused frown on their faces. Billy turned towards us and acknowledged our claps with a quick nod.

Daddy picked up his bible and walked out as we all followed. This was clearly the most uncomfortable memorial service I had ever attended. I was furthest from the aisle, so I was the last one to leave of our family. Lawrence, in front of me, took his sweet time, strolling slowly and gazing at the casket as he left. I wanted out of there. *'Walk, walk, walk!'* I thought, trying not to step on his heels. I glanced towards the Klansmen, but my eyes settled on Billy. He was sitting with his head down. He glanced up at me. I thought I saw tears in his eyes. It was the first time I saw Billy without anger.

Finally, I was out of the room. I saw the funeral director shaking hands with Daddy. "Thank you for coming," he mumbled so no one would hear. "I'll be seeing you."

"Not too soon, I hope!" Daddy said loudly, before walking out the door.

As we arrived back home from the funeral, Mamma stopped me in the front yard.

"I have something to show you," Mamma said excitedly. "C'mon, Betty, you slowpoke!" She was already on the top step of the porch before I knew it, as she gestured for me to hurry. "We've been waiting for you," she gasped.

'We?' I thought. *'Oh, Lord. What's Mamma up to now? Did she get a puppy?'*

I walked into the front door and looked. Sitting on the sofa were two little black girls, twelve and fourteen-years-old. They had on pretty dresses and ribbons in their sleek, black hair that shined like a raven's. They smiled nervously, as they held each other's hand.

"This, here, is Susanna and Victoria," Mamma said proudly. "And we adopted them!"

I was so shocked that my first verbal reaction was probably inappropriate. But I was tired. Ephraim, Lawrence, and Esther had moved out of the larger home, but I asked the question anyway.

"Where they gonna' sleep?"

Without missing a beat, Mamma answered joyfully, "I gave them your room."

I smiled at the girls, threw out a "Nice to meet you", and darted towards my bedroom. Sure enough, my bed had been moved back into the same room as Evelyn June's.

'Why doesn't anyone check with me about anything?' I wondered.

But I walked back in, knelt down in front of the cute sisters, and looked at both of them. "Welcome," I whispered with sincerity.

They both beamed huge smiles.

It turns out that Mamma had found a ministry of helping other children. It undoubtedly assisted her with finding peace after losing her own three boys and a grandson. As a matter of fact, if the Division of Family Services had a lieutenant, it was Mamma. If she knew a child anywhere who needed a home, she found someone who gave them one.

Susanna and Victoria were two sisters from nearby Excelsior Springs, whose mother had tragically died. They quickly became family. A few years later, Victoria began to date Dan, and they became inseparable. Susanna eventually met and married a man from Plattsburg. His name was David Hayes, and they moved to a town called Higginsville.

My mom continued helping other homeless kids, always providing them with warmth, love, and a hot meal, along with a future home. I never knew who might be temporarily staying the night on a bed, a sofa, or even the floor, but we always made room. Our home became the transition home. But the one thing Mamma became known for was treating every child the same.

And, oh, how she changed lives...

"I can't stop thinking, Betty," Mamma told me one evening on the front porch, as the cool breeze drifted through the scented pines. "If I don't stay busy, I think about George, Butchy, Josh, Jr., and little Tony."

A teardrop fell from her face. I hadn't seen Mamma cry in a long time.

"If I don't call on God and stay busy..." She cropped her hand midair for a second. "I begin to think... 'specially 'bout George..."

Right about now was the perfect time to tell Mamma about my most recent dream.

"Mamma," I began, ever so softly. "God gave me a dream."

"Please tell me about it," Mamma said, wiping away the tear.

"Butchy, Josh, Jr., and little Tony were walking up a road," I said. I watched Mamma's eyes squint into the breeze, and I knew she was picturing the vision as I spoke. She rocked in her chair and smiled.

"They came up to this big, huge gate," I went on. "But it wasn't no normal kind of gate... It was this really big pearl thing. And it opened. Then this exquisite Man came out. His hands and his feet were brown like polished brass... so dark and beautiful. He had holes in his wrists and welts on his back that you could see through his brilliant white robe. He was leading them through the gates of heaven. When He turned around, I saw George standing right behind Him, trying to peek around to see what newcomers were coming in."

Mamma gasped, smiled, and cried at the same time.

"But George was still discussing his facts, Mamma," I continued. "He was standing up straight, healed from his condition, and speaking all those crazy truths again. And, after everyone walked in.... the big pearl gate started closing behind them... Little Tony gave George one of those sloppy kisses that Butchy used to give when George bent down to hug him. And George started giving them all a tour of heaven spoutin' a buncha' facts like some kinda' tour guide!"

Mamma took a deep breath. "Knowing George, that tour is still going on..." She closed her eyes and laughed heartily.

The soft breeze moved her gray-streaked hair, gray much too soon from a lifetime of pain and heartache. The setting sun now shined on her face. She finally seemed at peace. She spoke not a word as the sunset disappeared. She rocked and smiled, smiled and rocked...

In perfect silence, she continued to rock.

Stop the unnecessary noise... and listen.

The time for love is now.

The time for peace is now.

The time to start truly living your days on this earth is now...

Before your set time comes...

Before your judgment comes...

Later that summer of 1973, Mamma died peacefully at the age of 63-years-old. After all her heart had been through, it finally gave out. Her appointed time came the same way it comes for all of us.

It seemed fitting to me that, as she lay on her deathbed, all of us saw a silhouette of an angel, a woman, on the wall right above her. She was wearing a large hat. Our "gift" again allowed us to see her personal escort. The angel stayed there approximately five minutes... and then disappeared. At that time, the soul of Mamma Sarena Jackson simultaneously left with her heavenly escort.

We cried... We rejoiced... Then... We wept...

At Mamma's funeral I sang. But my song was not the same. When a parent dies, inwardly, the Spirit whispers to you, "You are next". Your generation is next. You no longer sit in the world as a relaxed spectator. Your seat becomes more uncomfortable. You are next. Your sound has more magnitude, more passion, more desperation... because you can now see the end. "Let me sing it clearly, let me sing it right. Let me sing it with grace. And hear me..." Especially in black lives, where a song can be so short. "Please hear me..." And your song, no matter how relaxed and joyous it starts, ultimately and irreversibly, reaches its crescendo.

And then its climax. And finally, forcefully, it moves towards its end. And you can't stop it. Once you begin your song... It's always moving towards its end.

And, somewhere in the middle, due to the very nature of songs, your song becomes unique and different...

You live again.

Let go of all bitterness... forgive.

Be patient, be brave, fight for peace, follow the loving ways of the Lord... *OVERCOME.*

Respectfully,

Betty Josephine Jackson

18

"The Final Chapter"

Not long after the fire, after the funeral, and while his daughters fought for their lives, Daddy Joshua Jackson rummaged through the last of the charred remnants of his home. He carefully gathered what was left. Now just ashes remained to be carried away to the dump. It was a sad irony that he had to transport his own doom. He was in no hurry. As he drove his last load to the landfill, he added it to the mass of trash previously dumped by others. As he had done hundreds of times, Joshua searched through the recent garbage. But now he especially intended to find usable odds and ends after losing everything in the fire. As he thoroughly searched, something horrible caught his eye.

As Daddy moved closer to inspect, he picked up a skull that somehow he knew belonged to one of his murdered sons... His heart sank. Before long, he spotted another one. No wonder the city leaders had insisted on closed caskets that were never to be opened under any circumstances. They hadn't even bothered to search for the dead. They had bull-dozed the three bodies towards the curb with the rest of the trash. Those in charge had callously tossed the remains of his sons and grandson into the landfill along with the other trash for the week.

Daddy took the skulls to the Cameron Police Department, and he never heard anything about the case again.

This would be the last of a generation of lies.

On December 20th, 2016, like all before me, and all after me, my time, too, had come. I died and was buried in Cameron, Missouri.

I had no regrets. I lived to tell my story.

There is a strength in our People that is as unique and exceptional as the most treasured of earthly stones, having been refined in the furnace of affliction for thousands of years.

They called us darkies. But we are the first ones called by the greatest Light.

In my numbered days, the faceless baby of my dreams had found its identity.

Stand mighty oaks. The time of your drooping like the willows is ended. The winds of change now breathe across every horizon. When God breathed Life into the dry bones, He didn't do it for our survival... He did it for us to be an exceeding great army in the last days.

And that, my brothers and sisters, is my last message to you.

Before I passed into eternity, however, I guess I had a little of Mamma in me. I couldn't have children of my own, so I adopted and raised a beautiful little girl, who would grow into a strong, black, Hebrew woman.

I named her Hope.

About the Author

Thomas A. Briscoe was born and raised in the old Northeast area of Kansas City, Missouri. He attended the University of Missouri-Kansas City earning a degree in Psychology and English Writing. Thomas has always had a passion for activism against discrimination, particularly in unfair practices that involve civil rights. Today he is an advocate for racial and disability equality. Thomas and his wife Stephanie have been married 27 years, raised six children, and now have six grandchildren. He still ministers and writes in his spare time.

Betty Jackson: born July 19, 1933 and died December 20, 2016

Joshua Jackson: born June 2, 1896 and died January 22, 1982

CPSIA information can be obtained
at www.ICGtesting.com
Printed in the USA
BVHW091343210621
610125BV00014B/2941/J